Philosophical Method: A Very Short Introduction

VERY SHORT INTRODUCTIONS are for anyone wanting a stimulating and accessible way into a new subject. They are written by experts, and have been translated into more than 45 different languages.

The series began in 1995, and now covers a wide variety of topics in every discipline. The VSI library currently contains over 650 volumes—a Very Short Introduction to everything from Psychology and Philosophy of Science to American History and Relativity—and continues to grow in every subject area.

Very Short Introductions available now:

ABOLITIONISM Richard S. Newman
THE ABRAHAMIC RELIGIONS
    Charles L. Cohen
ACCOUNTING Christopher Nobes
ADAM SMITH Christopher J. Berry
ADOLESCENCE Peter K. Smith
ADVERTISING Winston Fletcher
AERIAL WARFARE Frank Ledwidge
AESTHETICS Bence Nanay
AFRICAN AMERICAN RELIGION
    Eddie S. Glaude, Jr
AFRICAN HISTORY John Parker and
    Richard Rathbone
AFRICAN POLITICS Ian Taylor
AFRICAN RELIGIONS
    Jacob K. Olupona
AGEING Nancy A. Pachana
AGNOSTICISM Robin Le Poidevin
AGRICULTURE Paul Brassley and
    Richard Soffe
ALBERT CAMUS Oliver Gloag
ALEXANDER THE GREAT
    Hugh Bowden
ALGEBRA Peter M. Higgins
AMERICAN BUSINESS HISTORY
    Walter A. Friedman
AMERICAN CULTURAL HISTORY
    Eric Avila
AMERICAN FOREIGN RELATIONS
    Andrew Preston
AMERICAN HISTORY Paul S. Boyer
AMERICAN IMMIGRATION
    David A. Gerber
AMERICAN LEGAL HISTORY
    G. Edward White

AMERICAN NAVAL HISTORY
    Craig L. Symonds
AMERICAN POLITICAL HISTORY
    Donald Critchlow
AMERICAN POLITICAL PARTIES
    AND ELECTIONS L. Sandy Maisel
AMERICAN POLITICS
    Richard M. Valelly
THE AMERICAN PRESIDENCY
    Charles O. Jones
THE AMERICAN REVOLUTION
    Robert J. Allison
AMERICAN SLAVERY
    Heather Andrea Williams
THE AMERICAN WEST Stephen Aron
AMERICAN WOMEN'S HISTORY
    Susan Ware
ANAESTHESIA Aidan O'Donnell
ANALYTIC PHILOSOPHY
    Michael Beaney
ANARCHISM Colin Ward
ANCIENT ASSYRIA Karen Radner
ANCIENT EGYPT Ian Shaw
ANCIENT EGYPTIAN ART AND
    ARCHITECTURE Christina Riggs
ANCIENT GREECE Paul Cartledge
THE ANCIENT NEAR EAST
    Amanda H. Podany
ANCIENT PHILOSOPHY Julia Annas
ANCIENT WARFARE Harry Sidebottom
ANGELS David Albert Jones
ANGLICANISM Mark Chapman
THE ANGLO-SAXON AGE John Blair
ANIMAL BEHAVIOUR
    Tristram D. Wyatt

Available soon:

For more information visit our website

www.oup.com/vsi/

Timothy Williamson

PHILOSOPHICAL METHOD

A Very Short Introduction

OXFORD
UNIVERSITY PRESS

OXFORD
UNIVERSITY PRESS

Great Clarendon Street, Oxford, OX2 6DP,
United Kingdom

Oxford University Press is a department of the University of Oxford.
It furthers the University's objective of excellence in research, scholarship,
and education by publishing worldwide. Oxford is a registered trade mark of
Oxford University Press in the UK and in certain other countries

First published in hardback as *Doing Philosophy* in 2018
First published as a Very Short Introduction in 2020

Impression: 1

Published in the United States of America by Oxford University Press
198 Madison Avenue, New York, NY 10016, United States of America

British Library Cataloguing in Publication Data

Data available

Library of Congress Control Number: 2020935143

ISBN 978-0-19-881000-1

Printed in Great Britain by
Ashford Colour Press Ltd, Gosport, Hampshire

Links to third party websites are provided by Oxford in good faith and
for information only. Oxford disclaims any responsibility for the materials
contained in any third party website referenced in this work.

Contents

Preface

I owe many thanks to the people who have helped in the development of this book at various stages with their perceptive comments: Jennifer Nagel, Peter Momtchiloff, Andrea Keegan, and Jenny Nugée at Oxford University Press; the anonymous referees; above all, my wife Ana Mladenović Williamson.

In a few places, I have put more technical details of an idea in a display box. Some readers will find them helpful, but they can be skipped without breaking the flow of the main argument.

List of illustrations

Chapter 1
Introduction

Jean-Pierre Rives is a rugby union legend. Livewire captain of the great French team in the years 1978–84, he was an unforgettably dashing figure on the field with long, wild, blond hair and often a bloodstained shirt. In a newspaper interview, he explained his thinking about tactics. The key, he said, is to have a clear and distinct idea of what you are trying to achieve. Then you should break each complicated move down into its simplest components, make them intuitive, and build it back up from there. Without naming the iconic French philosopher René Descartes (1596–1650), Rives was following both his signature emphasis on the need for clear and distinct ideas and one of his *Rules for the Direction of the Mind* (rule 5). French schools teach philosophy, and it has unexpected uses.

Philosophy also has dangers. Rives did not recommend another part of Descartes's method, his radical strategy of doubting whatever he could, including the whole world outside his mind, in order to rebuild science on the firm foundation of the few remaining certainties. Extreme doubt may not yield sporting success. Anyway, Descartes did not live up to his own high standards. He relied on dodgy old ways of thinking to 'prove' God's existence and then used God to resolve his doubts. Even at the time, many philosophers found his solution unconvincing. His reasons for doubt were like Frankenstein's monster, which he constructed but could not control. That is the problem of scepticism. It's often dismissed as a non-issue, of interest only to paranoid philosophers. But don't forget the public relations consultants called in by politicians and businesses to undermine inconvenient scientific discoveries, like global warming and the harmful effects of smoking. Those consultants have a slogan: "Our product is doubt". They know they can't prove the scientists wrong. Their aim is just to create enough confusion, to make people think "The experts can't agree, so there's no point worrying". Climate change scepticism isn't a harmless philosophical eccentricity; it's a threat to future generations.

Descartes's starting point for reconstructing knowledge was his knowledge of his own inner thought. That too still has strange echoes. In March 2003 the United States under President George W. Bush and the United Kingdom under Prime Minister Tony Blair invaded Iraq and overthrew Saddam Hussein's regime, claiming that it had weapons of mass destruction (WMD). The claim soon turned out to be false. In a 2004 speech defending his actions, Tony Blair said: "I only know what I believe". He hadn't known that there were WMD, but he had known that *he believed that* there were WMD. He tried to divert attention away from the question of testable evidence out there for WMD to the question of his inner sincerity.

Philosophy also plays a role when we recognize that the people of that region have endured a long history of human rights abuses. We can do so because we have an idea of human rights. Philosophers played a key role in developing that idea: notably, in the same period as Descartes, Hugo Grotius (1583–1645), John Locke (1632–1704), and others.

Philosophy isn't something totally alien to us; it's there already in our lives, in trivial ways and important ones. But what *is* philosophy? What are philosophers trying to achieve?

Traditionally, philosophers have wanted to understand the nature of *everything*, in a very general way: existence and non-existence, possibility and necessity; the world of common sense, the world of natural science, the world of mathematics; parts and wholes, space and time, cause and effect, mind and matter. They want to understand our understanding itself: knowledge and ignorance, belief and doubt, appearance and reality, truth and falsity, thought and language, reason and emotion. They want to understand and judge what we do with that understanding: action and intention, means and ends, good and bad, right and wrong, fact and value, pleasure and pain, beauty and ugliness, life and death, and more. Philosophy is hyper-ambitious.

That brief description raises an obvious question: since scientists study many of those topics, how is philosophy related to science? They were not always separate. From the ancient Greeks on, philosophy included *natural philosophy*, the study of the natural world. To cut a long story short, through the 16th and 17th centuries, natural philosophy turned into something recognizable as natural science in the modern sense, especially physics. Pioneers such as Galileo and Newton still described themselves as natural philosophers. Some philosophers were also scientists and mathematicians, including Descartes and Gottfried Wilhelm Leibniz (1646–1716). But natural philosophy or natural science developed a distinctive methodology, with a key role for experimentation, exact observation using special instruments such as telescopes and microscopes, measurement, and calculation. Increasingly, this child of philosophy has looked like a rival and mortal threat to its parent. For philosophy and natural science seem to be in competition to answer the same questions about the underlying nature of reality. If it is a duel, philosophy seems to be outgunned, for it only has thought, while natural science has those other methods too. If philosophers insist that they are better at thinking than natural scientists, who will believe them? To change the metaphor, the philosopher is cast in the role of the lazy man lecturing us from the comfort of his armchair about how the universe must be, while the scientist goes out to look and see how it really is. If that's right, isn't philosophy obsolete? Thus the rise of modern natural science has provoked a slow-burning crisis of philosophical method.

Much of the subsequent history of philosophy can be interpreted as a series of responses to that crisis of method, attempts to find something, *anything*, that philosophical methods can do better than scientific ones. Those attempts have often involved drastically scaling down the ambitions of philosophy, as later chapters will explain.

In my view, the supposed opposition between philosophy and science assumes an overly narrow, one-size-fits-all conception of science. After all, mathematics is just as scientific as natural sciences like physics, chemistry, and biology, all of which constantly rely on it, yet mathematicians don't do experiments. Like philosophers, they can work by thinking in an armchair. This book explains how the methods philosophers use are the appropriate scientific methods for answering their questions, which are questions of the traditional ambitious kind. Like mathematics, philosophy is a non-natural science. Unlike mathematics, it is not yet a fully mature science.

Admittedly, many contemporary philosophers are anything but scientific in their approach. This book is about doing philosophy *well*, not about doing it badly, though what counts as doing it well is itself contested. Many philosophers will hate my picture of how to do philosophy. I leave the reader to judge.

This book explains how philosophy can answer questions of stupendous generality. It involves nothing exotic, no altered states of consciousness. The reader may sometimes react: "But I do that already!" That's exactly the point. Philosophy, like all science, starts with ways of knowing and thinking all normal humans have, and applies them a bit more carefully, a bit more systematically, a bit more critically, iterating that process over and over again. Through the contributions of thousands of men and women over thousands of years, it has taken us to places of the intellect no one person, unaided, could ever have reached. Most people, especially children, from time to time ask themselves questions containing seeds of philosophy, just as most people ask themselves questions with seeds of physics, biology, psychology, linguistics, history.... The great difficulty is in identifying and providing the conditions for those seeds to grow. Without those conditions, each generation is stuck with lots of seed and no fruit.

I have been doing philosophy for well over forty years. It is still one of my greatest sources of pleasure—and frustration. I hope that this book will convey some of the pleasure, and not too much of the frustration.

Chapter 2
Starting from common sense

Common sense in philosophy

There is a story of a traveller who asks the way to somewhere and is told, "If I were going there, I wouldn't start from here". The advice is useless because one has no choice but to start from where one is. The same applies to any inquiry. We have no choice but to start from the knowledge and beliefs we already have, and the methods we already have for getting new knowledge and beliefs. In a phrase, we have to start from *common sense*. Of course, that doesn't mean we have to *end* at common sense. We hope to go far beyond it. But can we ever completely escape our reliance on common sense? Don't we bring it with us on our journey?

Imagine someone suffering from continual hallucinations. He can't rely on his own experience. He can't even rely on others' reports of their experience, because he may be hallucinating those 'reports' too. He is in no fit state to participate in any natural science. Thus even the most sophisticated natural scientists must presuppose that their senses have not gone haywire. At least to that extent, they still rely on common-sense ways of knowing.

Just like natural science, philosophy never completely escapes its origins in common sense. Some philosophers have been firm defenders of common sense, or at least much of the common sense of their own time and place. Examples are Aristotle (384–322 BCE), Thomas Reid (1710–96), and G.E. Moore (1873–1958). Others seek to escape what they see as its errors, though never with total success. Whereas natural scientists tend to leave their reliance on common-sense methods in the background, simply taken for granted, philosophers are more likely to foreground it, often because they are not quite easy about its status. This recurrent, self-conscious engagement with common sense, asserted or questioned, is one aspect of philosophical method.

What is common sense?

What does common sense include? Humans start with more or less the same cognitive capacities (there are exceptions, of course). We can look and see. We can listen and hear. We can touch and feel. We can lick and taste. We can sniff and smell. We can manipulate. We can search. We can remember. We can imagine. We can compare. We can think. We can communicate our thoughts to others in words and pictures, and understand what they say and show to us. In such ways, we learn about our environment, each other, and ourselves. We come to know the world of which we are part. Much of that knowledge comes naturally or casually as we grow up and live in the world, even without formal education at school or university.

By 'common-sense' knowledge in a society I mean whatever most of its members know. Thus common-sense knowledge varies from one society to another. In modern societies, it's common-sense knowledge that the sun is much larger than the earth. In Stone Age societies, that wasn't common-sense knowledge. In a Serbian-speaking society, it's common-sense knowledge that the word 'crveno' means *red*. In other societies, that isn't common-sense knowledge, because few of their members understand Serbian. But not all common-sense knowledge varies so much. In every human society it's common-sense knowledge that people have heads and blood.

Common-sense *beliefs* in a society are whatever most of its members *believe*. All common-sense knowledge may be common-sense belief, but not all common-sense belief is common-sense knowledge. For if a belief is false, it isn't knowledge. In an isolated society where everyone believes that the earth is flat, they don't *know* that it's flat, simply because it isn't. They may *believe* that they know that it's flat, but that belief is false too. Similarly, in a racist society, most members have false beliefs about people of other races. They are common-sense beliefs in that society, but not common-sense knowledge, simply because they are false, so not knowledge at all. Even if members of that society *believe* that their common-sense beliefs about other races are common-sense knowledge, that further belief is false too. It's hard to distinguish between common-sense knowledge and common-sense belief in one's own society, but often members of another society can tell the difference.

I'll apply the phrase 'common sense' not only to common-sense knowledge and common-sense belief in a society, but also to the usual ways of thinking which produce that knowledge and belief.

Common-sense questions, philosophical questions

Humans, like many other animals, are curious. We want to know. It's good to have lots of knowledge. It comes in handy in all sorts of unpredictable ways.

Common-sense thinking includes asking all sorts of questions. Many concern quite particular matters. Where's the milk? Who's that over there? Others have more generality. How do you make cheese? How long do mice live? Others are more general still. They include 'what is' questions. A child drinking a mug of milk may ask, "What is milk?" She knows well enough how to apply the word 'milk', but she still wants to know *what milk is*. She may be told how milk comes from cows, and mothers. In that case, an answer is already common knowledge in her society. In other cases, the answer may not yet be common knowledge, or even common belief. For instance, some people may ask, "What is honey?", knowing that it can be found in bees' nests but not how it got there. They may ask, "What is water?", for instance when puzzled by how it can freeze to ice and unfreeze again. Science begins with such questions, as well as with questions about the properties of specific kinds of plants and animals. They are not questions about words or concepts in our minds, but about the stuff itself: milk, honey, water. We can't eat or drink words or concepts.

The questions continue. What are the sun and the moon? What is fire? What is light? What is sound? There is no natural division between such questions, which we now regard as the beginnings of science, and questions we now regard as the beginnings of philosophy. What is space? What is time? Those questions are asked in both physics and metaphysics, the branch of philosophy concerned with reality as a whole, not in totally different senses, though they may get very different answers. Natural science began as natural philosophy (see Chapter 1).

'What is' questions go back to the beginning of philosophy. Plato (429?–347 BCE) asked, "What is justice?" and "What is knowledge?"—still central philosophical questions. He was not asking about the (ancient Greek) words or concepts, but about justice and knowledge themselves. Of course, they are not *stuff* like milk, honey, or water. You can't have a pint of justice or a kilo of knowledge. But that is not a difference between philosophy and natural science. Biology answers the question, "What is life?" (and many others), but life is not a stuff. You can't have a pint or kilo of life. There's a distinction between living and non-living things; one task for biology is to explain the underlying difference. Similarly, there's a distinction between just and unjust actions; one task for philosophy (specifically, political philosophy) is to explain the underlying difference. There's a distinction between

9

knowledge and ignorance; another task for philosophy (specifically, epistemology) is to explain that underlying difference too. Common sense recognizes life, justice, and knowledge. Our natural curiosity can make us want to understand them better.

Of course, thinking about common-sense distinctions sometimes makes us dissatisfied with them. The ordinary words with which we draw them may be too vague, or muddle together several different distinctions, or mark only superficial differences. That can happen in both philosophy and natural science. We may need to introduce new terminology to mark clearer or deeper distinctions and create a more helpful framework for further investigation. Common sense is the starting point, not the end point.

Common sense as a check on philosophy

Common sense is not a mere point of departure for philosophy to leave behind. It remains in another role, as a check on the philosopher's provisional *conclusions*.

I once had a colleague who presented his theory of perception in a lecture. A student pointed out that the theory entailed that it is impossible to see through a window. My colleague's theory was refuted by the common-sense knowledge that it *is* possible to see through a window. I see trees through one as I write.

Any theory inconsistent with common-sense knowledge is false. For whatever is known is the case, so whatever it is inconsistent with is *not* the case. Another example: metaphysicians such as John McTaggart (1866–1925) have argued that time is unreal, meaning that nothing happens after anything else. That is inconsistent with the common-sense knowledge that people often eat breakfast after they get up. Thus the metaphysical theory is refuted. Contemporary philosophers often rule out philosophical theories by showing them to be inconsistent with common-sense knowledge.

There's an obvious worry about using common sense as a standard by which to judge philosophical theories. What if we are mistaking a false common-sense belief for common-sense knowledge? In some societies, they believe 'Torture is not wrong'; indeed, they believe 'We all know that torture is not wrong'. Philosophers in such a society may think they have refuted a theory of human rights by showing it to be inconsistent with common-sense knowledge, because it implies that torture is wrong. Isn't that 'refutation' deluded?

The worry is that appeals to common sense are just a disguise for reliance on popular prejudice in judging philosophical theories. Such suspicions are especially strong amongst philosophers with views inspired by modern science, because they regard common sense as pre-scientific. Bertrand Russell (1872–1970) called it 'the metaphysics of savages'. For instance, on the basis of Einstein's theory of special relativity, some philosophers deny that the present is more real than the past and future; they will not be impressed by appeals against them to common sense. They regard it as embodying an out-of-date understanding of time and space.

Another theory inconsistent with common-sense belief says that there are only atoms (or fundamental particles) in the void. Some philosophers controversially take that to be a lesson of modern science. On their view, there are really no such things as the large-scale objects of common sense: no sticks and stones, no tables and chairs. Although there *appear* to be large-scale objects, *really* there are none. But now the dangers in a radical rejection of common sense start to emerge. For *to whom* do there appear to be large-scale objects? To us humans, presumably. Things don't appear any way to a fundamental particle, since it has no mind. But humans are large-scale objects too, so, on the radical view, there are no humans; thus it doesn't even *appear* to anyone that there are sticks and stones. Nor is it merely convenient to use words like 'stick' and 'stone', since there is no one to use them; indeed, there are no words, since words are not fundamental particles. Isn't this getting out of hand?

There is an issue here for natural science as well as for philosophy. Natural science is rooted in our capacity to make observations. If a scientific theory implies that there is nothing capable of making observations, isn't it cutting off the branch it's sitting on? Even if one tries postulating observations without an observer, they too would involve large-scale events of the sort being denied. A theory is self-undermining if it is incompatible with the possibility of obtaining evidence in its favour. That goes for theories both in natural science and in philosophy. Since obtaining such evidence ultimately depends on common-sense methods of knowing through the senses, there's a limit to how far defensible theories can disagree with common sense.

The disputed role of common sense as a check on philosophical theorizing raises a more general question: what kind of evidence have we to go on in philosophy?

Fallibility about evidence

Many philosophers treat *appearances* as the gold standard of evidence by which to judge theories in both natural science and philosophy. On their view, a good theory must *save the appearances*. In other words, it should accurately predict how things will appear to us—or at least, avoid inaccurately predicting those appearances. Now a theory can accurately predict the appearances yet still say that those appearances are false. For instance, it can predict that the moon will look to us much larger than the stars, and consistently add that the moon is really much smaller than the stars. A more radical theory may even predict that it will look to you as if there is a moon much larger than the stars, while adding that really there are no stars and no moon out there at all, there are only figments of your imagination. What the theory must not predict is that the moon will *look to us* much smaller than the stars. If saving the appearances suffices for fitting the evidence, then ultimately, the only evidence you have to go on right now is how things appear to you right now. Whether you are seeing the stars and moon or merely hallucinating them, your evidence includes the fact that it *appears to you as if* there are stars and a much larger moon.

Why equate our evidence with how things appear to us? What makes the equation appealing is this thought: I may be wrong about how things really are, but at least I'm not wrong about how they *appear* to me. But are we really infallible about how things appear to us?

To use appearances as evidence for or against a theory, it isn't enough that they simply *happen*. For instance, a theory predicts that, if you do a particular experiment, a spot will appear to move. Once you do the experiment, using the result for or against the theory requires you to *judge* whether a spot did indeed appear to move. Judgements can be right or wrong. We humans are fallible in making judgements even about how things appear to us. If no spot appears to move, I may still convince myself otherwise because I'm committed to the theory, and make the biased judgement "A spot appeared to move". Whatever our evidence is, we are fallible in making judgements about it. Sometimes we get it wrong. Even if we do our best to counteract our unconscious biases, we may fail. Thus there is a flaw in the argument, "My only evidence is appearances to me, because I can be wrong about everything else", because it sets a standard for evidence that not even those appearances meet.

In any case, equating evidence with appearances runs contrary to the spirit of science. That spirit requires evidence to be checkable, repeatable, open to scrutiny by others. Momentary appearances to one person do badly on all those tests. In that respect, common sense does better, because it is shared and can be checked. What papers in scientific journals cite as evidence are the actual results of experiments, described in large-scale physical terms. Such descriptions are more precise and technical than descriptions of our surroundings in everyday terms, but closer to them than to descriptions merely of how things appeared to someone.

The case of natural science suggests that the quest for a kind of evidence about which we are infallible is a wild goose chase. *Whatever* evidence is, what we treat as evidence will sometimes turn out to be false. No scientific procedures are designed to provide 100 per cent guarantees against error in practice. Rather, they are designed to facilitate the correction of errors in the long run. That is the best to which philosophy too can aspire.

Both philosophy and natural science must rely in multiple ways on our ordinary human capacities to learn about the world in common-sense ways. Both must therefore develop strategies for responding to the danger that what we have treated as knowledge is in fact false. The human condition means that we cannot rely on prevention alone, for occasional errors are bound to creep in, despite our best efforts. We also need methods for diagnosing and curing errors in what we treat as our evidence *after* they have occurred. In practice, therefore, we must allow a right of appeal against supposed evidence. But such a right does not imply that as soon as anyone questions a piece of supposed evidence, we stop treating it as evidence. That would make unsupported challenges decisive, which would allow a mischievous sceptic to bring both philosophy and natural science grinding to a halt, just by mechanically questioning whatever was produced as evidence. Rather, to deserve to be taken seriously, the critic must offer good reasons for doubting a specific piece of supposed evidence. Those reasons themselves had better be based on evidence, which can in turn be questioned. Chapter 3 will discuss such disputes in more detail.

The reliability of common sense

On the picture sketched in this chapter, if common sense is totally out of touch with reality, then neither philosophy nor natural science has much chance of putting us in touch with reality, since both are ultimately too reliant on common-sense methods of knowing. But isn't the assumption that common sense is *not* totally out of touch with reality rather optimistic? For won't common-sense beliefs have evolved to be *practically useful* rather than true, or even approximately true? And don't the differences in common sense between one society or time and another suggest that their common senses do not mirror reality?

Those sceptical arguments are unsound. First, true beliefs tend to be more practically useful than false beliefs. Second, we tend to find disagreements in common sense more surprising and so more interesting than agreements, which were expected and so are boring. Since our attention is on the disagreements, we are likely to overestimate the extent of disagreement compared to all the background agreement. Experience suggests that any two groups of humans in contact with each other will manage to communicate: the differences in common sense are not too deep for communication.

If one seeks actual cases of 'common sense' achieving practical usefulness without truth, the best place to look would be at non-human animals, for human vanity or solidarity does not prejudice us in their favour. Think of a leopard stalking a herd of impalas. Both species surely have their own 'common-sense' ways of learning about their environment (see Figure 1). Is it plausible that those ways are totally out of touch with reality? Not at all. For both leopards and impalas, it is literally a matter of life and death to know whether there's a member of the other species nearby and, if so, where. They have evolved to be good at acquiring such knowledge. We can often explain why a particular leopard or

1. Leopard and impalas.

impala acts as it does by attributing just such knowledge to it. Of course, like us, they are fallible, and sometimes have false beliefs. An impala may falsely believe that no leopard is nearby. But what explains the error is the leopard's skill or luck, not the impala's total detachment from reality. Naturally, leopards' and impalas' knowledge mainly concerns the tiny fraction of reality of practical interest to them, but within those limits it is impressive. It certainly impressed me when I watched impalas interacting with a leopard in South Africa.

It is biologically implausible to deny common-sense knowledge to non-human animals. It is just as biologically implausible to deny common-sense knowledge to human animals. Ascribing such knowledge involves no favouritism towards ourselves. There is good evidence for it.

The practice of testing philosophical theories against common-sense knowledge is thus quite reasonable. So too is the practice of challenging alleged cases of common-sense knowledge given specific grounds for doing so. It can be hard in practice to say just what should count as part of our evidence. But the same goes for natural science too: evidence is always in principle open to challenge.

Chapter 3
Disputing

Two sides of an argument

Conferences on philosophy have much in common with academic conferences on anything else. But in one way they differ. Amongst philosophers, a lecture often matters less than what follows—'Q&A', the question-and-answer period. That is when the speaker's arguments and conclusions are put to the test. Questioners propose counterexamples, allege fallacies, discern ambiguities. In response, the speaker fights for the life of their cherished ideas. Exchanges continue, back and forth, over several turns. The rest of the audience watches and listens keenly, as if following a chess match, trying to work out who's winning. Sometimes a draw is offered with the words "It's a stand-off" and tacitly accepted; sometimes the chair intervenes to cut short a stalemate. There is a code of signals to the chair: a raised hand means a new question, a raised finger a follow-up on the current point. A serious conference may schedule an hour for Q&A after each talk.

When it comes to the outcome, the chess analogy is misleading, since it suggests that, once the exchange is over, it's always clear who won. But the rules of argument are much less clear than the rules of chess, and can themselves be disputed, so two sides may disagree on the legitimacy or effect of a move. The chair is no umpire or referee, and doesn't rule on such matters. There may be no consensus on who had the better of the exchange. Perceptions can depend on prior theoretical commitments. Indeed, the exchange may itself have been partly or wholly on the legitimacy of moves in the lecture.

Some philosophers are unhappy with this model of philosophical discussion as gladiatorial combat. Those who lack the confidence to step into the arena are consigned to the passive role of mere spectators, yet self-confidence is not highly correlated with insight. What has single combat to do with the search for truth? There is something to such worries. When the philosophical climate goes bad, aggressive bluster or suave sophistry can silence careful reasoning. But to discourage sharp-edged questions only exacerbates matters, by making it easier for high-prestige speakers to bluff, and get away with bad arguments.

If the emperor has no clothes, everyone should feel entitled to say so. I once heard a lecture by a well-known scholar of the philosopher Friedrich Nietzsche (1844–1900), urging that Nietzsche's philosophy is not mere academic theorizing; if taken seriously, it transforms one's life into something radically different and unconventional. In Q&A, an undergraduate asked him how come in that case he was a professor of philosophy delivering an academic lecture in the conventional way to a student philosophy society. The Nietzsche scholar was huffily dismissive: "I don't see the relevance of that question". Everyone else in the room did. The emperor may not enjoy being told he has no clothes, but he can still benefit; he may even take the radical step of getting some. As for the Nietzsche scholar, twenty years on he remains a professor of philosophy in the same respectable department, regularly publishing academic volumes on his usual themes.

Admittedly, I gave a very partial view of philosophical discussion. I presented it as a zero-sum game, where one party's gain always equals the other party's loss. Many exchanges in Q&A are straightforwardly cooperative. Audience members may suggest additional evidence for the speaker's idea, or new applications of it, or ways to generalize it, or modifications of it in the spirit of the speaker's aims, or ways to simplify a supporting argument. The threat of an objection does not always lurk behind a request for clarification.

Nevertheless, the phenomenon of two sides arguing *against* each other is too central to philosophical practice to be dismissed as misbehaviour. Moreover, it is connected with the starting point of philosophy. For how is one to discover the limitations of one's common sense, and get beyond them? A natural answer is: by meeting someone whose common sense is in conflict with one's own. By arguing with each other, both sides have the opportunity to test the strengths and weaknesses of their starting points.

In politics, it is sometimes wise to brush disagreements under the carpet, since the alternative may be disunity or even violence. Intellectual inquiry does not flourish under those conditions. It requires relevant disagreements to be got out into the open, not muffled up. I have occasionally experienced philosophical cultures in which hard criticism was frowned on. They were deeply hierarchical: those lower down the hierarchy were not supposed to question those higher up. It is an ideal habitat for error.

A feel-good slogan is that discussion should be constructive, not destructive. It sounds like a platitude, but imagine telling city planners that they should always build houses and never knock them down. What happens when space is in short supply and filling up with bad housing? In philosophy, good and bad ideas compete for attention, which is also in limited supply. Of course, the slogan that discussion should be destructive, not constructive, would be far worse, but we need to get beyond such simplistic slogans if we are to understand better what kinds of discussion will help us most to answer philosophical questions correctly.

Adversarial philosophy

A useful comparison is with the adversarial system for settling legal disputes. Each side has an advocate, to argue its case as strongly and effectively as possible. In a criminal trial, there is the prosecution and the defence. This is one widespread format for getting at the truth in cases of disagreement. The idea is to ensure that each side gets a fair hearing. For that to work properly, each side must be competently represented, by someone willing and able to find and present the favourable evidence and arguments. The system has obvious disadvantages, for instance when one side is more competently represented than the other. But it also has advantages over the system of the single investigating magistrate. For even the fairest of magistrates is still human, and may reach premature conclusions, become demotivated from pursuing alternative lines of inquiry, and so miss the truth. The adversarial system is well designed to provide adequate motivation for each side of the argument. Similar considerations apply to philosophical disputes. Although lawyers argue on the side that pays them, while philosophers usually argue on the side of their intellectual sympathies, both have strong incentives to argue well.

Like defence and prosecution lawyers, philosophers often argue for what others see as a lost cause. The reason is different, though: typically, they become over-attached to their own ideas. This is not a peculiarity of philosophers: it is a natural human trait. With pardonable exaggeration, the great physicist Max Planck said that truth triumphs in science not because its opponents are won over, but because they die. Such obstinacy is not all bad; it ensures that ideas are given every chance to overcome criticisms, rather than being abandoned prematurely. When two senior philosophers argue some issue out with each other in public, with prestige at stake, it is often clear that neither of them will ever persuade the other; even so, it is not a waste of time if there are uncommitted students in the audience, making up their own minds as to which of the two is having the better of the argument.

Sometimes, even more like lawyers, philosophers argue on behalf of an idea they do not really believe in, just because they think it deserves to be taken seriously.

The legal comparison reminds us that court cases, under both adversarial and non-adversarial systems, often result in unjust verdicts. The challenge is to find specific changes in procedure that would make such verdicts less likely—just saying that courts must proceed constructively would not help. Similarly, error often triumphs over truth in philosophical debate. The challenge is to find specific changes in procedure that would make such results less likely. I wish I knew how to meet that challenge.

The adversarial system requires a judge and perhaps jury to adjudicate between the two sides, to reach a decision. In philosophy, there is less urgency about reaching a decision than in the courts, but insofar as anything plays the role of judge and jury, it is the wider community of philosophers. The first requirement for it to play that role is a disposition to listen carefully to what all parties say. The second requirement is an appreciation of the rules of argument. I know many philosophical communities that do well—though very far from perfectly—on both scores. Because such virtues are prized, each generation tends to learn them from its predecessors. Of course, they are by no means exclusive to philosophy. Education by its nature favours and inculcates the ability to attend carefully to what is said. Likewise, education and experience in any academic discipline foster appreciation of the rules of the types of argument characteristic of that discipline—for instance, in the case of mathematics, the rules of mathematical proof. In philosophy, interpersonal disputation plays such a large role that philosophers unsurprisingly tend to have an unusually sensitive appreciation of its underlying rules.

When careful listening and appreciation of the rules of argument are widespread in a community, bullying, bluff, and sophistry are typically counterproductive, because they make the perpetrator look stupid. There is a corresponding incentive for those with good points to make them, because they can expect to be listened to.

Naturally, there is also the fear that, if you make what feels to you like a good point, it may be found out by others to be a bad point after all. Some level of such a fear is no bad thing, since it comes with a capacity for self-criticism and a respect for the intelligence of others. But too much fear is paralysing. What can help is that philosophers experienced in listening carefully and applying the rules of argument learn how *hard* philosophy is, how easy it is for even the best philosophers to go wrong, and so are less inclined to judge someone on the basis of one misfire.

To say that a philosophical culture of interpersonal argumentation encourages competition instead of cooperation is like saying that a chess club encourages competition instead of cooperation. There's some truth in it, but it's a facile contrast. Chess is a competitive game, with one player winning if and only if the other loses, but the club itself is a cooperative venture of its members, and even a single game of chess involves cooperation between the players, because both want to play, for pleasure or reputation or to improve at chess. Similarly, although there are winners and losers in some philosophical disputes, the institution of philosophy is a cooperative venture of philosophers, and even a single philosophical dispute involves cooperation between the disputants because both want to argue the point. Indeed, although chess does not primarily aim at knowledge in the way philosophy may primarily aim at knowledge, games of chess do in fact add to knowledge, for instance of which positions are wins for black. Similarly, philosophical disputes add to knowledge, at the very least of which philosophical positions are defensible. Both philosophers in a dispute may improve their theories as a result, even if they still disagree.

Logic games

There is nothing new about the role of interpersonal dispute as a medium for philosophy. In medieval scholastic philosophy, oral disputations were formalized as a sort of game, *obligationes*, played in Latin, with rules almost as formal as those of chess (see Figure 2). One side had to argue for a statement, the other side against it, in accordance with the strict rules of medieval logic, most of which are still recognized as valid. Each side had to be explicit about which of the other side's premises (assumptions) they accepted, and which they rejected. They could distinguish several senses of a premise, accepting it in some, rejecting it in others. Someone senior would act as umpire, to ensure that the rules were properly applied. The spirit of the game is still recognizable to modern philosophers, even though the details of the rules now look too restrictive, because modern logic has identified many valid forms of reasoning irreducible to the forms studied in medieval logic.

There are also logic games with rules more closely related to modern logic. They typically involve two players—a defender and an attacker—and a statement in dispute (see Box 1 if you want more details). If the statement is true, the defender has a winning strategy. If the statement is false, the attacker has a winning strategy. Thus if both players make the best moves available to them, the defender will win if the statement is true, and the attacker will win if the statement is false: the outcome of the game corresponds to the truth-value of the statement. Such games show the naivety of a general contrast between games and the search for truth, since their rules are designed precisely to serve the search for truth.

Of course, most philosophical discussion is *much* less formally structured than a logic game. Nevertheless, such games provide a

2. University masters in a disputation over the definition of happiness, with an audience of students, from a 13th-century Parisian copy of a commentary on Aristotle's *Nicomachean Ethics*.

Box 1 Rules in a logic game

If the statement in dispute is 'Everything is so-and-so', the attacker chooses an object, gives it a name 'N', and the game continues with 'N is so-and-so' as the new statement in dispute ('so-and-so' could be anything, for instance 'green'). The attacker gets to choose because it only takes one counterexample to falsify (show false) an 'every' statement, and the attacker is the one who needs to find it.

If the statement in dispute is 'Something is so-and-so', the defender chooses an object, gives it a name 'N', and the game continues with 'N is so-and-so' as the new statement in dispute. The defender gets to choose because it only takes one example to verify (show true) a 'some' statement, and the defender is the one who needs to find it.

If the statement in dispute is 'A and B', the attacker either chooses 'A' or chooses 'B', and the game continues with the chosen one as the new statement in dispute ('A' and 'B' could be any statements, for instance 'It's raining' and 'It's cold'). The attacker gets to choose because it only takes one false component to falsify an 'and' statement, and the attacker is the one who needs to find it.

If the statement in dispute is 'A or B', the defender either chooses 'A' or chooses 'B', and the game continues with the chosen one as the new statement in dispute. The defender gets to choose because it only takes one true component to verify an 'or' statement, and the defender is the one who needs to find it.

If the statement in dispute is 'Not A', the defender and the attacker swop roles and the game continues with 'A' as the new statement in dispute (for instance, if 'A' is 'It's raining', 'Not A' is 'It's not raining'). The reason for the role-swopping is that the truth of 'Not A' is equivalent to the falsity of 'A', and the falsity of

'Not A' is equivalent to the truth of 'A', so the defender of 'Not A' should attack 'A' and the attacker of 'Not A' should defend 'A'.

Each move reduces the logical complexity of the statement in dispute. Sooner or later, the game reaches a point where what is in dispute is a logically simple statement. It is assumed that such statements can be verified or falsified by observation. If it is true, the defender wins. If it is false, the attacker wins.

good model of how, under suitable conditions, an adversarial framework can serve the pursuit of truth.

Dialogues

In less formal terms, the natural written form to represent philosophical disputes and question–answer exchanges is the dialogue. It's also one of the oldest forms of philosophical writing. Plato's dialogues are still the most famous and evocative examples of the genre. Despite that, Plato expressed disapproval of written philosophy, because one can't engage in question-and-answer with a book. Perhaps a written dialogue is the next best thing.

The Greeks also tended to pose philosophical paradoxes in question-and-answer form, where contemporary philosophers would present the deduction of an absurdity from plausible premises. An example is the sorites paradox, which shows the acute difficulty of applying vague terms soundly. The Greeks posed it as a long series of questions and answers:

Q: Do 10,000 grains make a heap?
A: Yes.
Q: Do 9,999 grains make a heap?
A: Yes.
Q: Do 9,998 grains make a heap?

And so on, in principle, all the way down to:

Q: Do 0 grains make a heap?

One gets that sinking feeling. To answer any question in the series differently from the next seems like treating the vague word 'heap' as more precise than it really is. Yet it is absurd to give all questions in the series the same answer, since the answer 'Yes' is obviously right for the first question and obviously wrong for the last one. However one answers, one looks and feels silly. By contrast, modern philosophers formulate the paradox as a deductive argument with two plausible-sounding premises:

Major premise   For every number n, if $n+1$ grains make a heap
                then n grains make a heap.
Minor premise   10,000 grains make a heap.

They then show how to reason step by step all the way down to the absurd:

Conclusion   0 grains make a heap.

The difference may not seem large, but it brings out how much the Greeks regarded doing philosophy as an interpersonal activity, not a solitary one.

Plato didn't put himself as a character into his own dialogues. His teacher Socrates appears, originally modelled on the historical Socrates. In the later dialogues, Plato used Socrates or another character as more of a mouthpiece for himself, but always with some distancing effect, so he could try out ideas without fully committing himself to them. Other philosophers have chosen the dialogue form to express views too dangerous for them to publicly endorse, by not officially identifying with the character closest to their own thinking. Even in what would now be classified as natural science, Galileo wrote his *Dialogue Concerning the Two*

Chief World Systems (1632) that way to distance himself from the heretical new sun-centred astronomy of Copernicus while still demonstrating its advantages over the traditional earth-centred astronomy of Aristotle and Ptolemy. The subterfuge failed: he made it too clear which side won the arguments, so the Roman Catholic Church banned the book and imprisoned him. David Hume did a slightly better job of concealing his subversive sympathies in *Dialogues Concerning Natural Religion* (1779), in his case scepticism about the existence of a god. Because he was suspected of atheism, he had been turned down for a professorship in philosophy at Edinburgh University in favour of a far less distinguished candidate. Gottfried Wilhelm Leibniz and George Berkeley (1685–1753) also wrote major works in dialogue form. With views closer to religious orthodoxy, they could make it clear which character they identified with, though the result was a loss of dramatic tension.

In general, the philosophical dialogue is a less pluralistic form than it looks: it has various characters but only one author. At worst, it is a dialogue between the ventriloquist and his puppet. In contemporary philosophy, it plays only a minor role. Logic formulas and footnotes are ill at ease in a dialogue. Nevertheless, the form retains significant strengths. For expository purposes, it embodies the interaction of different points of view in a vivid, memorable, and perspicuously structured way. A reader's emotions are more easily engaged by a dispute between imagined people than a logical inconsistency between abstract theories.

But doesn't philosophy require a coolly rational, objective, unemotional attitude? That's psychologically unrealistic. Even in science, humans perform best when strongly motivated. Burning curiosity is an emotion. When you don't care which of the answers to a question is right, you won't be alert to the subtle logical differences between them. If you like one character and dislike another, you scrutinize each move in their dialogue as a potential threat or opportunity. The emotions you feel may reveal to you the underlying philosophical instincts you had all along. Even the less savoury emotions associated with competitiveness, rivalry, and ambition can be harnessed to play a constructive role in natural science and philosophy when the disciplinary culture rewards good work over bad, valid arguments over invalid ones. We saw how that's possible in philosophical disputes.

The dialogue still has uses as a medium for philosophical research. Sometimes each side regards the other's theory as *nonsense*, rather than false. Thus one can't expound the theories from a neutral standpoint, for expounding a theory presupposes that it makes sense. In such cases, it's best to let each side speak for itself, which is in effect the dialogue form. An example is a current dispute in philosophical logic between 'generality absolutists', who say, "It makes sense to generalize about absolutely everything whatsoever, without restrictions", and 'generality relativists', who say, "However many things you generalize about, it always makes sense to generalize about even more". Each side regards the other's words as somehow self-undermining, failing to make the kind of sense they want to make.

Short of a proper dialogue, it is very common, having presented one's view, to give some potential objections to it with one's replies. It is a kind of hypothetical dialogue with the reader: "If you are tempted to make this objection, here is my reply". This often helps to clarify just what the view implies, and what it does not.

Discussions of scepticism often focus on imaginary dialogues with a sceptic. Contemporary epistemologists are much concerned with the vulnerability of common-sense ways of thinking and talking to sceptical objections. They dramatize it in mini-dialogues like this:

MARY: You don't know much about the animals in this zoo.
JOHN: That's not fair! I know the animal in this cage is a zebra.

MARY: For all you know, it's just a mule cleverly painted to look like a zebra. The zoo may be having financial difficulties.

JOHN: I suppose you're right. I was wrong. I don't know it's a zebra, after all.

Mary's next step could be to suggest that John doesn't even know that he's awake, because for all he knows he's asleep in bed, dreaming he's at the zoo.

The difficulty of John's position also shows something about the dangers of dialogue. For what should he say, in order not to concede Mary's point? If he says, "Come off it! You know as well as I do that it's a zebra", he will sound dogmatic and obtuse. Once your interlocutor has introduced a possibility, there's conversational pressure on you to take it seriously, not just dismiss it. The sceptic ruthlessly takes advantage of such etiquette to cut the ground away from under the non-sceptic's feet. The culture of philosophy supports those sceptical moves by its unusually tolerant attitude to bizarre possibilities.

John could reply to Mary, "Good point! But for present practical purposes, if you don't mind, I'll just assume I do know it's a zebra". That sounds more polite and accommodating. But in practice it will probably turn out just to be a more diplomatic way of not taking Mary's point seriously, as will emerge if Mary answers, "Actually, I do mind". If you are really unwilling to make assumptions your conversation partners won't grant, you hand them terrifying power over your own thought. Sceptics will be only too pleased to exploit that power to drag you into the sceptical pit with them. You had best be careful whom you talk to.

Chapter 4
Clarifying terms

It depends on what you mean

A mountain guide told me about a frustrating conversation he once had with a client who quoted a temperature in degrees. The guide asked, "Is that degrees Fahrenheit or degrees Celsius?" The man replied, "What do you mean? A degree is a degree". However much the difference between the two scales was explained to him, the man always repeated, "A degree is a degree". He felt on safe ground there. To him, any attempt to question that tautology sounded like a con trick. But sometimes, to make progress, we must clarify our terms.

If you ask a philosopher whether you have free will, you are unlikely to get a straight answer, "Yes" or "No". Instead, you may be told: "It depends what you mean by 'free will'. If you are asking whether your decisions cause your actions, surely they often do. If you are asking whether they are *uncaused* causes of your actions, surely not. Your decisions are caused by your beliefs and desires, and those beliefs and desires have causes of their own, and so on." If you feel you meant something else again by 'free will', the philosopher will discuss with you what that might be.

One of the best-known figures on British radio in the 20th century was a philosophy professor, C.E.M. Joad (1891–1953), a panellist on the popular programme *The Brains Trust* (see Figure 3). He

3. C.E.M. Joad, philosopher as media celebrity, 1940s style.

was famous for beginning his answers to listeners' questions with the words, "It all depends on what you mean by...". The stereotype of the philosopher became someone who asks "What do you mean?", instead of "How do you know?" That is the pop version of the trend in 20th-century philosophy often called the *linguistic turn* (see p. 35).

Many philosophers have hoped to make philosophy less disputatious by clarifying terms, and to escape from futile, deadlocked arguments. Perhaps the disputes are merely *verbal*. If one person says, "The temperature is 0 degrees" and another replies, "No, it's 32 degrees", they may think they are disagreeing, but if the first speaker means degrees Celsius and the second degrees Fahrenheit, there is underlying agreement about the temperature. Similarly, when philosopher A says, "We have free will" and philosopher B replies, "We have no free will", the verbal appearance of a dispute may mask underlying agreement, if they mean different things by 'free will'. If we notice an ambiguity, we can resolve it by introducing separate terms with the different meanings, perhaps 'A-free' for what A means and 'B-free' for what B means (if we can think of nothing better). Thus both A and B can happily say, "We have A-free will but no B-free will", not even appearing to disagree. Each side gets what it wants.

If we have to decide what to mean by a word, one definition may be more *useful* than another, but not more *true*. For instance, in mathematics it is more convenient to define the word 'prime' not to apply to the number 1, but making the opposite decision would not have led to false theorems, just to differently worded ones. According to Rudolf Carnap (1891–1970), when philosophers ask what sound like deep theoretical questions about the nature of reality, such as "Do numbers exist?", what is really at stake is a practical question about which language it would be most fruitful to speak, for scientific purposes. If scientists use a theoretical language in which the word 'number' is logically analogous to the word 'planet', will that help their work? Some languages can express more than others, but greater expressive power comes with costs as well as benefits: it may generate unmanageable complexity.

For Ludwig Wittgenstein (1889–1951), philosophical problems arise because our ordinary language exerts a deep pull on us towards confusions. For example, grammar suggests a misleading analogy between proper names—'the River Danube'—and numerical terms—'the number seven'—tempting us to think that numbers are just as much objects as rivers are, only more abstract. Then we wonder how we can think about things that are nowhere. But further investigation reveals ways in which the analogy between 'seven' and 'Danube' breaks down. "He interrupted seven times" makes sense; "He interrupted Danube times" does not.

Obviously, what interested Carnap and Wittgenstein was not the six-letter word 'number' itself. Most of the issues would survive translating it by another word in another language. That point is often put by saying that what matters is not the word 'number' but the concept *number*. Different words can express the same concept, or have the same meaning. For them, philosophy asks *conceptual* questions, not merely *verbal* ones. It clarifies concepts, sorts out conceptual confusions. In the 20th century, many philosophers held such views. Many still do. Naturally, those views influence how they do philosophy in practice.

Clarifying concepts: if that is philosophy's job description, it has something useful to do without attempting, hopelessly, to rival science. In that picture, philosophers put concepts into good working order, while others actually put them to work. The picture may also seem to legitimize the armchair way of doing philosophy, to explain why philosophers have no need to go out and look at the world or experiment on it. For they already possess the concepts under investigation, by their competence in a language that expresses them; either a natural language such as English or Mandarin, or an invented artificial notation defined by explicit rules. It's not like studying a foreign language from the outside.

In practice, hopes that this linguistic or conceptual turn would make philosophy less disputatious have been dashed. Identifying the unspoken rules of one's own language turns out to be very hard. If you have ever helped someone learn your native language, you have probably had the experience of knowing that something they said sounded wrong but without being able to explain to them *why*—what rule they had broken. First, second, and third guesses at the rules are typically wrong, even when made by trained linguists. Still, they can usually do better than people untrained in linguistics, sometimes by comparing your native language with other languages. Although significant progress in understanding the rules of one's native language can be made from the armchair, it's not a fully adequate method. If we switch from describing how words are currently used to saying how it might be helpful to use them in the future, things are just as controversial, because people disagree about what the effects would be, and whether they would be improvements.

An example is the recent bitter controversy about the word 'woman'. The standard definition was biological: a woman is an adult female human. But what about the social role of women— their moral and legal rights to get an education, to own property, or to vote, conventional expectations of their behaviour in sex, marriage, child-rearing, careers, and so on? Don't those have something to do with the concept *woman*? Is what matters their actual social role, or the role they are stereotyped as playing? If the latter, what happens when people in one society, say Britain, speak about women in another society, say Pakistan—is what matters the British stereotype of women or the Pakistani stereotype of women? And what about the currently influential idea that to be a woman is just to be willing to apply the term 'woman' to oneself? There is no easy answer to the question what concept or concepts the word 'woman' now expresses. As for the future use of the word, any proposal is explosive. For consider a biological male who identifies as a woman: if the proposal implies that we *should* call that person a 'woman', it will enrage many people, and if it implies that we should *not* call that person a 'woman', it will enrage many other people. The very idea of someone in authority telling ordinary people how they ought to use ordinary words like 'woman' is controversial too. Well-meaning professors tend to imagine linguistic reform being led by people like themselves, but in practice a trend towards redefining terms may favour more sinister causes—for instance, when 'torture' is redefined to exclude waterboarding. Politically, people habituated to going along with linguistic reforms are easier to manipulate.

Still, words sometimes need clarification. That applies to *all* forms of inquiry, not just to philosophy. For example, physicists distinguish two senses of the word 'mass': relativistic mass (defined in terms of total energy) and proper mass (defined in terms of non-kinetic energy). Confusing the two would lead to detectable errors. Similarly, historians who use the word 'feudalism' clarify how they understand it, because some societies in some periods count as 'feudal' by one definition but not by another. Neither physicists nor historians had to wait for philosophers to make the clarification for them. The need for it became plain to them as their subject developed. This raises the question: does conceptual clarification play a *special* role in philosophy, or does it just play more or less the same role there as it plays in all forms of serious inquiry?

Detecting ambiguity may play a larger and more systematic role in philosophy than in any other branch of inquiry, with the possible exception of literary criticism. Philosophers are trained to be alert to ambiguity. But so far that is a difference of degree, not kind. For physicists or historians, resolving unclarity in 'mass' or 'feudalism' is a *preliminary* to their main investigation, like cleaning a surgical knife before using it on a patient. The surprising claim is that, for philosophers, such clarification is not a preliminary to their main investigation but the main investigation itself. Can that claim be true?

The need to clarify 'mass' came from theoretical developments in physics, in particular Einstein's theory of special relativity. The need to clarify 'feudalism' came from developments in history—more detailed analyses of more societies in more periods. Where is the need for philosophers' clarifications supposed to come from, if all

37

they do is clarify? If they are just clarifying previous philosophy, wouldn't it be cheaper and easier to abolish philosophy altogether? Then there would be no philosophy in need of clarification. Even if people strayed into philosophizing from time to time, they would not be paid for it, and taxpayers' hard-earned money would not be wasted.

We can never expect to make our words *perfectly* precise. For in order to make one word more precise, we must use other words that are themselves to some extent vague, and that vagueness will infect our clarifications. Vagueness can sometimes be reduced, but it can never be eliminated, from either language or thought. Efforts at clarification should be concentrated where there is a special need for it. The need may be either theoretical or practical. There were special theoretical needs to clarify 'mass' and 'feudalism'. An example of a practical need for clarification is in law. A law simply against making a 'big mess' in a public place would be unworkable, because 'big mess' is so vague. The standard for counting as a 'big mess' would have to be made clearer (though not perfectly clear) for the term to be used in an effective law. Conceptual clarification cut off from such theoretical or practical needs is pointless.

Fans of philosophy as conceptual clarification sometimes suggest that it gives us understanding rather than knowledge. But that is a false dichotomy. If you don't *know* why the sky is blue, you don't *understand* why it is blue either. As you learn more—get more knowledge—about how Hannibal got his elephants over the Alps, you understand more about how he got them over. The idea of increasing understanding without increasing knowledge is an illusion, however tempting, in philosophy as everywhere else.

Often under the influence of Wittgenstein, some philosophers take themselves to be doing pure conceptual clarification, untainted by theoretical activity such as advancing hypotheses to be confirmed or falsified by future evidence. They regard such hypothesis-testing as characteristic of natural science, by contrast with philosophy. Their attitude tends to result in a peculiarly dogmatic style of philosophizing, since their conception of philosophy forbids them from properly acknowledging the possibility of clear-headed challenges to their own philosophical arguments, and in particular of the premises from which they start. If one thinks that one is simply clearing up confusions, one will tend to regard whoever opposes one's efforts as confused.

Here is an example. Some philosophers of mathematics hold that it studies mathematical objects, such as numbers or sets, which are not in space or time but are just as real as anything that is. That view is called *platonism*, because it resembles Plato's theory of abstract forms (the word is spelt with a lower-case 'p' because platonists don't try to follow Plato in detail). The most distinguished modern platonist was Kurt Gödel (1906–78), one of the greatest logicians of all time. Philosophers who take their job to be diagnosing confusion often accuse platonists of confusing the kind of meaning had by mathematical terms like 'the number 7' or 'the empty set' with the kind of meaning had by terms for ordinary objects in space and time, such as 'the River Danube' or 'the empty box', as we saw. Their diagnosis is that platonists naively assume that since we use 'the River Danube' and 'the empty box' to refer to objects, we must use 'the number 7' and 'the empty set' to refer to objects too. Those who make that patronizing diagnosis typically know far less logic and mathematics than the platonists whose view they are dismissing. Anyway, the evidence does not support their diagnosis. Most platonists do not feel forced into their view by linguistic analogies. Instead, like Gödel, they accept platonism because they find it crucial for the best explanation of what mathematicians are doing. Whether platonism is true or false, it is not based on mere confusion.

Concepts and conceptions

Is the concept of confusion itself confused? Does the concept of conceptual clarification need clarifying? The underlying problem is with the concept of a concept—or, to put it non-circularly, with the word 'concept'. Some of the difficulties came up with the word 'woman'. What does it take for two people to express the same concept with the word 'woman'? When as a student I first read about the philosopher Hilary Putnam, I assumed that Hilary Putnam was a woman—every Hilary I had met was female. When later I discovered that Hilary Putnam was a man, did my concept of a woman change, if only slightly? Did I mean something different by 'woman'? If every difference in the beliefs expressed using a word makes a difference to its meaning, it will be very hard for two people to mean the same by a word, or for one person to mean the same by it for more than a short time. I know whether there's a biro in my pocket; you don't know: does it follow that we don't mean exactly the same by 'biro'? If we pile all such information into concepts, we shall be unable to draw a useful distinction between conceptual and non-conceptual questions. That would undermine the idea that what is special about philosophy is that it asks conceptual questions.

A distinction is sometimes drawn between *concepts* and *conceptions*. A concept is more like a dictionary definition. For example, a dictionary may define the word 'vixen' as 'female fox', so the concept *vixen* just is the concept *female fox* (my dictionary also gives another definition for 'vixen', as 'quarrelsome woman', which would be another concept). By contrast, your conception of a vixen includes all the beliefs you would express using that word (in a given sense). Unlike the concept *vixen*, my conception of a vixen includes my belief that a vixen lives under my garden shed. Dictionaries are for concepts, encyclopaedias for conceptions. If we distinguish concepts from conceptions like this, then conceptual questions are special, because they concern definitions. Clarifying one's concepts is defining one's terms.

One advantage of distinguishing concepts from conceptions is that it explains how knowledge can be communicated from one person to another and preserved over time. Conceptions are personal and fleeting, but definitions can be shared and stable. 'Vixen' has been defined as 'female fox' for many centuries and many millions of speakers of English.

The view of concepts as definitions also underpins the idea of philosophy as conceptual analysis. If the concept *vixen* is the concept *female fox*, then we can analyse the concept *vixen* as a combination of the concept *female* with the concept *fox*. Of course, philosophers have not been particularly interested in the concept *vixen*, but they have hoped to find such analyses of more philosophically central concepts, like *knowledge*, *meaning*, and *causation*.

However, the dictionary definition model doesn't take us very far. Even for colour words like 'red', ordinary understanding has much less to do with a dictionary definition than with our ability to recognize examples of red as red when we see them. Most words are like that: who understands 'cat' or 'chair' or 'copper' by knowing a definition? If you can't recognize a cormorant by yourself, you can still use the word 'cormorant' because you are part of a community of English-speakers, some of whom are more expert than you. As competent speakers of English, we understand philosophically interesting words like 'know', 'mean', and 'cause', but not by knowing dictionary-style definitions of them. Philosophers' attempts to provide such definitions have a long track record of failure. Nevertheless, we can still recognize the difference between knowing where your keys are and not knowing, or between meaning by 'bank' the edge of a river and meaning a financial institution, or between causing the window to break and not doing so.

Most concept-lovers have recognized the inadequacy of the dictionary definition model. However, they still distinguish *conceptual truths* from other truths that are not conceptual, even if they are necessary. For example, 'Red things are coloured' is supposed to express a conceptual truth, because the connection has been somehow built into our concepts *red* and *coloured*. By contrast, in an isolated community where people can recognize whales by sight but everyone assumes them to be merely enormous fish, 'Whales are mammals' does not express a conceptual truth, because the connection has not been built into their concepts, even though being a mammal is in fact a necessary part of the nature of a whale. If philosophy's concern is with conceptual truths, that might help explain why philosophy can be done in an armchair.

How can we tell whether a truth is conceptual or not? One idea is that if a sentence expresses a conceptual truth, everyone who understands it will accept it. For example, everyone in our community who understands 'Red things are coloured' agrees with it, whereas people in the imagined community disagree with 'Whales are mammals'. But universal assent is too high a standard to help concept-lovers. For example, an intelligent native speaker of English might learn the words 'red' and 'coloured' in the usual way, but later decide that the word 'coloured' is so tainted by its racist associations that it correctly applies to nothing. She refuses to call anything 'coloured'. She no longer assents to 'Red things are coloured'; she instinctively rejects it, once she has grown accustomed to her new view. But she has not lost her understanding of the sentence; she has no difficulty in following other speakers when they use the word 'coloured' in the usual way. If there is one such dissident in the enormous community of English-speakers, 'Red things are coloured' fails the test of universal assent. Similar examples can be constructed for any candidate conceptual truth. It is unclear that any useful distinction between conceptual and non-conceptual truths can be drawn.

Clarifying and theorizing

Fortunately, the value of clarification does not depend on any distinction between conceptual and non-conceptual matters. Think again of mathematics, the clearest and most precise branch of human inquiry. Mathematicians often use explicit definitions. But if you trace their chains of definitions back, you always reach undefined terms—their definitions don't go round in circles or continue to infinity. In modern mathematics, those undefined terms typically belong to set theory, the standard framework. The main undefined term in mathematics is $\in$, the symbol for set membership: the formula $x \in y$ says that x (say, the number 7) belongs to the set y (say, the set of prime numbers). There are no standard mathematical definitions of 'belongs' or 'set'. Introductory textbooks gesture vaguely towards everyday talk of collections and the like, while admitting that such analogies are inadequate: the stamps in a stamp collection have to be collected together in a sense irrelevant to mathematics. But this lack of definition is no problem for mathematics. The reason is that mathematicians have a powerful *theory* of sets, with axioms giving plentiful information about what sets there are. For instance, one axiom says that for every set there is a set whose members are the subsets of the first set. Another axiom says that there is a set with infinitely many members. Another says that sets with the same members are identical, and so on. For most mathematical purposes, the theory gives mathematicians just what they need to reason clearly and rigorously about sets. The axioms are plausible but have no clear claim to count as *conceptual* truths. It is quite possible to understand what they say and still doubt them, though the success of modern mathematics is good evidence in their favour.

Some people try to turn the axioms of set theory into a definition of the term 'set-theoretic structure'. The idea is that a structure is 'set-theoretic' if it obeys all the axioms of set theory. But the attempt is pointless, for in order to put such a definition to work mathematicians would need a theory of *structures*, which would look remarkably like the theory of sets in disguise. No progress would have been made.

As a model for philosophy, basic mathematics is far more helpful than the dictionary. What we need for clear reasoning are not trivial 'truths by definition' but a strong, explicitly articulated theory. Clarity does not aim at a mythical standard of indubitability. Rather, its point is to make mistakes in our reasoning clearly visible, as they are in mathematics. If you hear someone deny the value of clarity, ask yourself why he might not want mistakes in reasoning to stand out clearly.

Chapter 5
Doing thought experiments

Use your imagination

Imagine someone seeing what looks just like smoke in the distance. He thinks: "There's a fire over there". He's right: there is a fire over there. But there's a catch. The fire hasn't yet started to smoke. It's just been lit to cook some meat. What he sees is really a cloud of flies, which have gathered because they smell the meat. Does he know there's a fire over there? He *believes* there's a fire over there, and he believes *truly*, because there *is* a fire over there. He also believes *reasonably*, in the sense that most reasonable people in his position, with his evidence, would form the same belief. But he doesn't seem to *know* that there's a fire over there. After all, he's right by luck. Perhaps the flies had gathered even before the fire was lit. So a belief can be both reasonable and true without amounting to knowledge.

That case was given by Dharmottara (around 740–800), a Buddhist philosopher who worked in Kashmir. He used it to show something important about the nature of knowledge. But his writings were unknown to philosophers in Europe and America. In the 1950s, the standard analysis of knowledge was as justified (reasonable) true belief. Then, quite independently of Dharmottara, the American philosopher Edmund Gettier came up with similar cases. In a short article published in 1963, he used them to refute the standard analysis of knowledge. The result was a revolution in epistemology, the theory of knowledge. The big question became: since knowledge is not mere justified true belief, what more is it? Dozens of alternative answers were proposed. One after another, they too fell victim to such counterexamples. The attempted analyses of knowledge had to become more and more complicated, as did the counterexamples to them. Perhaps we shouldn't try to analyse knowledge in terms of belief plus truth plus other factors, because knowledge is somehow more basic than belief.

Such episodes show how far philosophy can be inspired and guided by examples. A theory can sound plausible, even compelling, on first hearing, or even to generations of intelligent, highly trained thinkers, yet collapse when faced with an apt counterexample. If we don't confront them with difficult examples, we are not testing our theories properly. We are accepting them uncritically, making life too easy for ourselves.

A striking feature of many examples in philosophy is that they are *imaginary*. I don't know whether Dharmottara ever witnessed or heard of a real-life case like the one described. The point is: it doesn't matter. *We* have to imagine it, even if he didn't. If such a case never happened, still it clearly *could* have happened, which is all we need to show that reasonable true belief is not *sufficient* for knowledge: reasonable true belief without knowledge is *possible*. If someone applied for a large grant to set up Dharmottara-style cases in real life and trick people into thinking "There's a fire over there", it would be a waste of money, because the lesson of the case is already clear. You don't always have to make something actual to show that it is possible. I've never given a lecture holding a banana in my hand throughout, but I know I'm physically capable of doing it.

Dharmottara's example is a *thought experiment*. We imagine a trick case of reasonable true belief. The target philosophical theory predicts that it will be a case of knowledge. But, independently of the theory, it is clearly *not* a case of knowledge. Therefore, the theory is false.

Thought experiments have also played a major role in the development of recent moral philosophy. For instance, Judith Jarvis Thomson at the Massachusetts Institute of Technology devised a famous one to challenge the argument that *if* the foetus is a person, *then* it has a right to life and abortion is wrong. In a 1971 article, she compared the situation of a pregnant woman to this imaginary case: you wake up to find yourself back to back with a great violinist whose circulatory system has been plugged into yours so your kidneys purify his blood as well as your own. The Society of Music Lovers kidnapped you for this purpose because it was the only way to save the great violinist's life from a terrible kidney disease; no one else has exactly the right blood type. If he stays plugged into you for long enough (perhaps years), he will recover. Otherwise, he will die. The violinist is unquestionably a person, and so has a right to life. But does that mean you are morally obliged to let him stay plugged into you for as long as it takes him to recover? Although an exceptionally selfless person might agree to do that, don't you have a right to say, "I'm very sorry, but I have my own life to live, and I'm not willing to sacrifice a large chunk of it like this to save your life, so I'll get the doctor to unplug you"? If that response is permissible, despite the violinist's right to life, why isn't it permissible for a mother to have an abortion despite the foetus's right to life? Of course, other philosophers have looked for morally significant differences between Thomson's case and abortion, but her thought experiment took the debate forward by showing that just granting that the foetus is a person does not settle the issue about the morality of abortion. As with Dharmottara's example, the fact that Thomson's case is imaginary does not undermine her point. Not only would replicating it in real life be unethical, it wouldn't clarify the moral issues.

Thought experiments and real-life experiments

Although thought experiments are in widespread use, they can be made to sound like cheating. After all, physicists have to *do* their experiments, and observe the results. It's not enough for them just to *imagine* doing their experiment, and *imagine* observing the result. How come philosophers get away with just sitting in their armchairs and imagining it all?

Part of the answer is that philosophical theories typically claim that some generalization is necessary: it holds in all *possible* cases, not just in all *actual* ones. For instance, Gettier was criticizing philosophers who meant that there is no *possible* case of knowledge without reasonable true belief or reasonable true belief without knowledge. If he had been up against more modest philosophers who just said that there is no *actual* case of knowledge without reasonable true belief or reasonable true belief without knowledge, then to refute them he might indeed have needed to produce a real person who really had a reasonable true belief without knowledge. Philosophically, claims about all possible cases tend to be more revealing than claims restricted to actual cases, since the former show more about the underlying nature of what is at issue, such as knowledge. By contrast, a generalization about actual cases may be true just by misleading lucky coincidence. A fair coin may come up heads on all *actual* tosses, but not on all *possible* tosses.

Another part of the answer is that physicists as well as philosophers use thought experiments. In criticizing the theory that heavy things fall faster than light ones, Galileo challenges it with a thought experiment in which a heavy object and a light one are joined by a string and dropped from a tower: when the string pulls taut, the lighter object should retard the heavier one, yet together they form a still heavier object, which according to the theory should fall faster than either. Einstein too was inspired by a thought experiment: if he rode on a beam of light, what would he see?

We can go deeper by reflecting on how a theory is tested—*any* theory, in philosophy, physics, whatever. To test it properly, we have to work out its consequences, what it predicts about various possible situations. But there are infinitely many such scenarios—for instance, infinitely many possible arrangements of particles for a physicist to worry about, infinitely many possible morally relevant complexities for a philosopher to worry about, and so on. Obviously, no one can think about each possible case separately. Many of them will be unrewarding as tests of the theory, because it predicts nothing of interest about them. It's a tricky art to think up a scenario that makes a good test of the theory, because it predicts something of interest about that scenario. If the theory's prediction about the scenario turns out to be correct, that is serious evidence for the theory. If its prediction turns out to be incorrect, that is serious evidence against the theory. To think up the possible situation and work out what the theory predicts about it is already a thought experiment. It is easy to underestimate the difficulty of identifying appropriate scenarios, for once they are pointed out, they may be quite easy to understand. Often, the skill is in coming up with them in the first place.

A further step is to check whether the theory's prediction about the imagined scenario is correct. In natural science, that is famously done by actualizing the possible situation and observing the result—in other words, by doing a real-life experiment. It may be a myth that Galileo dropped balls of different masses from the Leaning Tower of Pisa to see whether they landed at the same time, but other scientists soon did similar experiments. However, actualizing the scenario is not the only way of testing a theory's prediction about it. What is needed is some reliable way, independent of the theory, to judge whether its prediction is correct. That may even be quite easy once we imagine the relevant scenario. For instance, without relying on any philosophical theory of knowledge, humans have some ability to recognize the difference between knowledge and ignorance in down-to-earth cases—for instance, who knows when you got up this morning and who doesn't. We can apply that ability to Dharmottara's down-to-earth thought experiment to recognize it as not a case of knowledge. Actualizing his possible situation is unnecessary.

Some thought experiments are easier to actualize than others. Galileo's is very easy to perform. Dharmottara's involves a more elaborate scenario, but is still realistic. Thomson's would require advances in medical science. Einstein's is physically impossible: one can't ride on a beam of light.

Some philosophers' thought experiments are much more far-out than Dharmottara's and Thomson's. The mythical ring of Gyges enables its wearer to become invisible whenever he wants; Plato uses it to explore how people would behave if they had no fear of being caught and punished for their crimes. In his attempt to show that mind cannot be reduced to matter, the contemporary Australian philosopher David Chalmers argues for the possibility of *zombies*, molecule-for-molecule replicas of us which nevertheless differ from us by having no conscious experience: all is dark within (see Figure 4). There is a difference between them and us, but not a *physical* difference.

4. **David Chalmers' zombie twin is the one on the left.**

If a thought experiment is used only as a stimulating mental exercise, the impossibility of the scenario may do no harm. Perhaps Plato's ring of invisibility and Einstein's ride on the light beam are like that. But when a thought experiment is used as a serious objection to a theory, it matters whether the scenario is possible. For instance, if some inconsistency were hidden in Dharmottara's story, it would not refute the theory that reasonable true belief is knowledge. If zombies are totally impossible, Chalmers cannot use them against theories that reduce mind to matter.

Knowing by imagining

How do we *know* whether a scenario is possible? When I read Dharmottara's story, I imagined the look of smoke in the distance, then closer up the meat sizzling over the newly lit fire, the flies buzzing round, and so on. Such events could obviously happen. What about zombies? Of course, I can imagine something that looks from the outside exactly like Dave Chalmers, sitting at a computer writing a book called *The Conscious Mind*. But to make it Chalmers' zombie twin, not Chalmers himself, I must also imagine that it has no conscious experience. I can't imagine that from the inside, for a zombie has no inside in that sense; it has grey matter in its head but no conscious point of view. If I imagine darkness, am I not imagining having a conscious experience of darkness, which by definition a zombie lacks? From the outside, I just have to say to myself, "It has no conscious experience", a rather minimal kind of imagining. Indeed, many philosophers deny that zombies are possible. They hold that a molecule-for-molecule replica of Chalmers would be just as conscious as the original. Although the definition of a zombie may be logically consistent, that is not enough to make zombies genuinely possible. There is no purely logical contradiction in the hypothesis that you *are* the number 7, but it is still impossible. No number could have been *you*. Perhaps there is a similar non-logical impossibility in the hypothesis of zombies.

Sometimes it's hard to tell which hypotheses are possible, which impossible. That is a problem for some thought experiments—but not for all. The possibility of Dharmottara's scenario is beyond reasonable doubt. Through imagining it properly, we know that it is possible. Also through our imagination, we can learn more about it. Crucially, we can come to know that, in such a scenario, the person who reasonably and rightly believes there's a fire over there doesn't *know* there's a fire over there.

At first, the idea of knowing by imagining may sound crazy. Isn't knowledge to do with *fact*, imagination with *fiction*? But that stereotype of the imagination is too simple. The human species did not evolve such an elaborate psychological capacity just so we can indulge our fantasies. When you think about it, you realize that a good imagination brings all sorts of practical rewards. For instance, it alerts us to future possibilities, so we can prepare for them in advance—guard against dangers, be prepared to take advantage of opportunities. As you enter a forest, it tells you there may be wolves, but also edible berries, to be on the look-out for. If you have a problem, your imagination may suggest possible solutions, such as different ways to cross the river that separates you from your destination.

We often use our imagination when choosing between several courses of action. For instance, if you have to choose between several places where you might spend the night, you may imagine what it would be like to spend the night in each of them, and decide on that basis. The imagination is especially useful when trial and error is too risky. Suppose that a broken cliff blocks your direction of travel. The cautious option is to take the long way round; that would be fairly safe but add an extra day to your journey. Best would be to climb the cliff, if you can, since that would take much less time and energy. Worst would be to try to climb the cliff but fail: with luck, you would be back where you started; with no luck, you would fall and be badly injured or killed. To resolve your dilemma, you may examine the cliff from a distance, to see whether you can imagine a possible route to the top: step by step, move by move, you try to imagine yourself climbing up, to see whether you would always encounter an obstacle you couldn't overcome. Of course, you *could* imagine a comfortable ladder miraculously appearing, but that would be pointless, since you know that in the circumstances no such ladder will appear. Instead, we are capable of a much more realistic sort of imagining, which is sensitive to what genuinely could happen in the circumstances. Through such realistic imagining you may learn whether you can climb the cliff, and whether if you tried you would succeed. You need such knowledge to make a wise choice between going round the long way and trying the cliff.

For practical purposes, a good imagination doesn't generate lots of possibilities; too many for you to think about. Instead, it generates a few possibilities; those it's most useful for you to think about—*practical* possibilities. Such an imagination improves your chances of survival. It is closely linked to the ability to predict the future. If you *see* someone starting across a rickety bridge, you may predict that it *will* collapse. Even if no one is starting across it, you may *imagine* yourself doing so, predict that it *would* collapse, decide not to try, and so save your life. In the long run, evolutionary pressures are likely to improve the accuracy and reliability of such imaginative exercises.

Imagining is our most basic way of learning about hypothetical possibilities. No wonder we use it in doing thought experiments. They are not some weird, self-indulgent thing only philosophers and a few other eccentrics do. Only the dumbest of animals would *not* think about hypothetical possibilities. When we do it, we usually do it in the normal human way, by using our imagination. Thought experimentation is just a slightly more elaborate, careful, and reflective version of that process, in the service of some theoretical investigation. Without it, human thought would be severely impoverished.

Intuition?

Unfortunately, some philosophers have described philosophical thought experiments in ways which make them sound much more exceptional and mysterious than they really are. When we judge that the man in Dharmottara's story doesn't know there's a fire over there, they say we are relying on an *intuition* that he doesn't know there's a fire over there. 'Intuition' sounds like some strange inner oracle, guiding or misguiding us from the depths.

To get clear about all this, the first step is to notice that such 'intuitions' are not confined to the imagination. As we saw, it makes little difference whether we judge "He doesn't know" when imagining a hypothetical scenario or when observing a real-life scenario of the same kind; the philosophical upshot is the same. According to fans of 'intuition', we are relying on an intuition that he doesn't know even when we make the judgement about a real-life case. What's more, on their view, we don't just use intuition for tricky cases; we use it in boringly straightforward, everyday cases too, for instance when you judge that a stranger you pass in the street knows whether you are walking but doesn't know whether you have coins in your pocket. It is also not supposed to matter whether the terms of the judgement happen to be ones philosophers are interested in. When you judge that the stranger you see is smartly dressed, you are still relying on intuition.

Do *all* judgements rely on intuition? That might make the category of intuition too broad and indiscriminate to be useful. Some philosophers try to narrow down the category by specifying that intuitive judgements (those based on intuition) are not inferred from evidence. But that restriction risks narrowing down the category too much. In a real-life Dharmottara case, the supposedly intuitive judgement "He doesn't know there's a fire over there" is based on evidence, such as the fact that he mistook a cloud of flies for smoke. In the corresponding imagined case, the same judgement made within the process of imagining has a similar basis. If basing a judgement in that way counts as inferring it from the evidence, then the key judgements in thought experiments *are* inferred from evidence, and so would not count as intuitive.

More promisingly, fans of intuition could narrow down the category by specifying that intuitive thinking is not based on a *conscious process* of inference. Thus, when I immediately judge "He doesn't know" in Dharmottara's story, my judgement counts as intuitive, for if there is a process of inference, I am not aware of it. By contrast, when I do a long mathematical calculation with pen and paper, I am aware of the process, so my answer does not count as intuitive. Drawing the line between intuitive and non-intuitive judgements in that way has a significant result: *all non-intuitive thinking relies on intuitive thinking*. For if non-intuitive thinking is traced back and back through the conscious processes of inference on which it was based, sooner or later one always comes to some thinking not itself based on a conscious process of inference, which therefore counts as intuitive thinking. Consequently, philosophy's reliance on intuitive thinking shows nothing special about philosophy, because *all* thinking relies on intuitive thinking. When physicists go through a conscious process of rigorous inference, making calculations and using observations, they are still relying on intuitive thinking, because even their thinking has to start somewhere. That does not make their thinking irrational; it just means that at least some intuitive thinking is part of rational thinking.

Recently, some philosophers have argued that philosophers *shouldn't* rely on intuitions. Others have argued that philosophers *don't* rely on intuitions. The debate rests on confusion about what 'intuitions' are supposed to be. However, most people agree that *if* philosophers rely on intuitions, they do so when giving verdicts on thought experiments, such as "He doesn't know". But when they try to say what is special about those verdicts, they come up with a kind of thinking on which all human thinking relies, as we just saw, so both the idea that philosophers shouldn't rely on it and the idea that they don't are non-starters.

Of course, none of this means that *all* 'intuitive' thinking is rational. Some of it is bigoted, dogmatic, and utterly wrong. If people's judgements of real-life cases are warped by prejudice, that prejudice is likely to warp their judgements of thought experiments too. For instance, someone who is indifferent to the suffering of animals in real life will probably manifest the same attitude when considering thought experiments about animal suffering.

Biases

Much recent scepticism about the reliability of philosophical thought experiments goes back to real-life experiments done by philosophers early in the century. They gave lots of non-philosophers some standard thought experiments and asked for their judgements. The results appeared to indicate that, for some thought experiments, people with East Asian cultural origins responded differently from people with European cultural origins, and women responded differently from men. In the philosophical tradition heavily reliant on thought experiments, they had mainly been judged by white males, but why should whites be any better than non-whites at judging thought experiments, or males any better than females?

More recently, however, such experiments have been redone many times, more carefully, with more involvement of fully trained psychologists, and the picture is now very different. The statistical differences between people of different ethnicities or genders have tended to disappear. The differences found earlier seem to have been the result of very subtle distortions in how people were selected for the experiments, which scenarios they were given, and so on—the sorts of easily overlooked confounding factors psychologists are trained to be on the lookout for, but philosophers are not. On the picture now emerging from the new evidence, the patterns underlying our reactions to philosophical thought experiments have far more to do with the cognitive capacities we humans share, irrespective of our ethnicity and gender. This is illustrated by the thought experiments with which I began the chapter. Dharmottara was a Buddhist in 8th-century Kashmir; I am non-religious in 21st-century Britain. Judith Jarvis Thomson is a woman; I am a man. Nevertheless, I find their thought experiments compelling.

That's not the end of the story. After all, even if all humans agree on something, that doesn't make it *true*. For example, if all humans agree that humans are the smartest creatures in the universe, it doesn't follow that we *are* the smartest creatures in the universe. What if we all give the same verdict on a thought experiment, but that verdict is wrong? Although the way we use our imaginations in evaluating thought experiments will tend to be reliable, for reasons discussed earlier, there is no reason to expect it to be 100 per cent reliable—quite the opposite. We often make mistakes in judging real-life cases; why should we be immune to them in judging thought experiments? This isn't a reason for not using thought experiments, for all human faculties are fallible. Rather, it's a reason for spreading our bets, not relying *exclusively* on thought experiments. If we use other methods too, they may help us catch our occasional mistakes in judging thought experiments, even if those mistakes are species-wide. Developing systematic general theories, supported by the evidence, is a good way of doing that. If we develop a systematic general theory about the possibilities for life to develop on any planet, supported by the evidence, we may come to realize how unlikely we are to be the smartest creatures in the universe.

In the long run, cognitive science, including the movement known as 'X-phi' (experimental philosophy), may cast light on inherent biases in human thinking, and so help us resist them, in ourselves as well as others. That hope is not restricted to biases in philosophy. Thinking in philosophy is too like thinking in other fields. It is not remotely plausible that we have any inherent bias whose distorting effects manifest themselves in philosophy but not in any other field of inquiry.

Chapter 6
Comparing theories

Theories of everything

Theories in philosophy, like theories elsewhere, are answers to questions. Of course, we rarely dignify the answers to easy questions by calling them theories: "Where's the breadknife?" "Over there". But, in a murder investigation, detectives may form the theory that the missing breadknife is in a nearby wood. Scientists' questions are usually more general, and philosophers' questions are amongst the most general of all.

Before any distinction was drawn between philosophy and natural science, people asked "What is the world made of?" Thales (around 600 BCE), supposedly the first Greek philosopher, answered: "Water". A closely related question is whether everything is made of matter, in short, "Is everything material?" The answer "Yes" to that question is the theory of *materialism* (not in the popular sense of caring only about wealth!). There were materialist philosophers in ancient Greece, India, and China. Later materialists included Thomas Hobbes (1588–1679) and Karl Marx (1818–83).

Strictly interpreted, materialism is inconsistent with modern science, which recognizes electromagnetic fields, spacetime, and much else that's not really matter. In contemporary philosophy, materialism has therefore been replaced by *physicalism*, which says that everything is physical. 'Physical' here means whatever laws of physics govern, including electromagnetic fields and spacetime as well as matter. Physicalists say: take the world as described by physics; that's it, there's nothing else. Of course, they don't expect *today's* physics to be the last word. Physics continues to progress; current theories will surely turn out to be incomplete and incorrect in various ways, and get replaced by better theories in the future. Physicalists allow for such developments, for by "laws of physics" they *don't* mean "what today's physicists take to be laws of physics". Amongst recent philosophers, a leading physicalist was Willard Van Orman Quine (1908–2000).

You might wonder why physicalism belongs to philosophy rather than to physics itself. The reason is the total generality of 'everything' in stating the theory. For instance, if there are numbers, then 'everything' includes them, so physicalism implies that numbers are physical. If there are minds, then 'everything' includes them too, so physicalism implies that minds are physical. But "Are numbers physical?" and "Are minds physical?" are not questions in physics. By themselves, the mathematical and experimental methods of physics don't answer them. Those methods don't tell us whether there are questions and answers beyond their reach. The people who grapple with such issues are philosophers.

Whether physicalism is true or false, it is one answer to questions central to our understanding of the world we live in, including ourselves. Is there more to reality than physics, or natural science more generally, can discover? Although physicists can do physics without worrying about that question, humanity as a whole would be sadly incurious and unreflective if we never thought about it. Nor is just vaguely wondering enough; shouldn't we at least *try* to answer it? Of course, anyone can *say* "Yes" or "No" to physicalism; what we need are good reasons to give one answer rather than the other. Once we

seek them, we are doing philosophy. A life that never engages
with philosophical theories is not fully reflective or inquiring.

Testing theories by thought experiment

Thought experiments can be used to test philosophical theories.
For instance, Chalmers' thought experiment about zombies is a
challenge to physicalism. Take your conscious experience of
waking up one morning, how it felt to you. Physicalism implies
that any such experience is physical. Some physicalists would
make sense of that by identifying your experiences with physical
events in your brain, neurons firing in a complex pattern. But
exactly similar physical events would occur in your zombie twin's
brain; neurons would fire in the very same pattern. You had the
conscious experience of waking up that morning; by definition,
your zombie twin did not. How it felt to you wasn't how it would
feel to the zombie, for nothing feels *any* way to a zombie. Thus,
Chalmers argues, your conscious experience was distinct from the
physical events in your brain. By a generalization of the argument,
your conscious experience was distinct from anything physical
whatsoever. It's a counterexample to the physicalist theory,
something non-physical. So Chalmers rejects physicalism as false.

How can physicalists respond to the zombie argument? They
usually argue that the apparent possibility of zombies is an
illusion. Your conscious experience of waking up is just the
physical event in your brain; one without the other is impossible.
Thus your zombie twin is impossible. But in that case, when we
try to imagine it, why does it *seem* possible?

A physicalist may explain why zombies *seem* possible like this.
There are two ways to imagine something happening to someone:
we can imagine it either from the inside, from that person's point
of view, or from the outside, from an external observer's point of
view. For instance, when I imagine someone waking up from the
inside, I may imagine a vague confused feeling, a sensation of

lying flat, and the grudging thought "I'm waking up". By contrast, when I imagine someone waking up from the outside, I may imagine the sight of a body stirring in a bed on the other side of the room, and the relieved thought "She's waking up". Obviously, we can imagine in either of the two ways without imagining in the other. So we can imagine from the outside someone waking up without imagining it from the inside. We can even add to the scene a brain scanner recording events in her brain. Finally, we can add the description in words: "She feels nothing; she has no conscious experience; she's a zombie". But, the physicalist argues, that does not enable you to know that zombies are genuinely possible: even if conscious experiences *were* just brain events, you could still imagine from the outside without imagining from the inside. Thus the physicalist explains away the apparent possibility of zombies as a predictable illusion created by the mismatch between two ways of imagining an event.

That does not silence anti-physicalists. Some of them argue that if zombies were really impossible, there would be a logical contradiction in the idea of a zombie, but we cannot find one.

Physicalists may retort that not all impossibilities are logical contradictions; some are in the nature of things themselves. For instance, you cannot possibly be the number 7, even though there is no purely *logical* contradiction in the idea that you are the number 7. The debate continues.

One moral of the zombie case is that we should not expect to do philosophy by thought experiments alone. For disputes can arise over what a thought experiment shows. They raise further questions, for example about the nature of possibility itself, which require a more theoretical discussion.

Fortunately, the zombie case is not typical of thought experiments in philosophy. There is widespread agreement about the results of many other thought experiments. They lack the problematic feature of the zombie case; its exploitation of a mismatch between two ways of imagining. Still, to avoid an attitude of uncritical acceptance, we must be on the lookout for such problematic features of thought experiments. That requires us to have a wider theoretical perspective on what we are doing when we assess them and their potential pitfalls.

All this may sound very different from testing theories by experiment in natural science. On the stereotype of that process, a scientific theory entails a prediction about what we shall observe in a certain experiment. We do the experiment and observe. If the observed result is what the theory predicted, the theory is confirmed. If what we observe is not what the theory predicted, the theory is refuted. It all sounds cut and dried, with none of the argumentative to-and-fro around philosophical thought experiments.

The stereotype grossly oversimplifies the process of testing scientific theories by experiment. There are at least two reasons for that.

First, by themselves many scientific theories don't entail observable predictions at all. The theories are formulated as mathematical equations too abstract to connect directly with observation. To get observable predictions from such a theory, scientists must combine it with 'bridge' principles linking its abstract terms to more concrete, observable ones. They also need auxiliary assumptions about how the experimental apparatus works, otherwise it might not measure what they intend. Often, to work out predictions, the scientists must also make various simplifying assumptions, which hold approximately at best—otherwise the calculations are too complicated, even for a computer. Thus, if the prediction turns out to be incorrect, the theory may not be to blame. The fault may be in one of the other principles and assumptions on which the scientists relied in working out the prediction, or they may simply have miscalculated.

Second, all sorts of thing can go wrong in doing the experiment itself. Scientists and laboratory technicians are human; sometimes they make mistakes. Equipment malfunctions; samples get contaminated. Consequently, scientists are more confident once the experiment has been done independently in several different laboratories, perhaps in slightly different ways, with the same result. The prediction may be correct about the experiment done right but incorrect about the experiment done wrong.

In short, testing a scientific theory by experiment is usually a messy, complicated business. The result is often much less cut-and-dried than the stereotype suggests.

Despite all this, experiments are still vital sources of scientific knowledge. The point is just how hard and complicated it is to get that knowledge; how much room there is for argumentative to-and-fro. Despite all the obvious differences between real-life experiments in natural science and thought experiments in philosophy, something they have in common is that they leave room for disagreement: it often takes more than one failed prediction to refute a theory, to eliminate the possibility that something other than the theory itself is to blame for what went wrong.

Rival theories

Rather than testing a single theory in isolation, scientists often *compare* rival theories, different answers to the same question, against each other. Which of them best explains the evidence? The same happens in philosophy. For instance, rather than testing physicalism in isolation, philosophers compare it with rival theories.

Someone might say that whenever a theory is tested, it's tested against the rival theory that simply denies the first theory. For instance, Einstein's special theory of relativity (STR) would be tested against the negative theory anti-STR, which simply says "STR is wrong". Similarly, physicalism would be tested against the negative theory anti-physicalism, which simply says "Not everything is physical". But such negative theories come too cheap. In just denying a general theory, they tell us nothing about *where* it goes wrong. By itself, anti-STR offers no alternative explanation of the experimental and observational data that STR explains. Similarly, mere anti-physicalism says nothing positive about what the non-physical things are. Roughly speaking, a serious rival theory should give different answers to the same questions. In some tricky cases, the rival may reject some of the very questions the first theory answers, but then it should explain why those questions deserve rejection. Rival theories should be informative.

An informative rival to physicalism is *dualism*, which postulates two main kinds of thing: mental and physical. Thought is mental and non-physical; matter is physical and non-mental. As a child, I used the word "mental" to mean *mad*, but here it means *mind-like*, just as "material" means *matter-like*. Descartes put dualism centre stage in philosophy, and it still has advocates.

It is hard for physicalists to disagree with the dualist claim that something is mental. After all, if they try to dismiss the mental as an illusion, they lose, because illusions themselves are mental. Instead, most contemporary physicalists accept that thoughts and feelings are mental but insist that they are *also* physical (if you want a more precise map of the alternatives, see Box 2).

For its fans, the zombie thought experiment makes more sense in dualist than physicalist terms: conscious experience is something mental, not physical, which you have and your zombie twin lacks. Even if the thought experiment does not conclusively refute physicalism, dualists may see it as *evidence* for dualism against physicalism. But, for its critics, the thought experiment gives no reason to view zombies as possible, so no evidence for dualism.

Box 2 Rival theories of mind and body

Physicalism is this claim: Everything is physical.

Dualism is the conjunction of these four claims:

[1] Everything is either mental or physical.
[2] Nothing is both mental and physical.
[3] Something is mental.
[4] Something is physical.

Panpsychism is this claim: Everything is mental.

Dualism is inconsistent with physicalism, because [2] and [3] together imply that not everything is physical. Thus physicalists must decide whether to deny [2] or [3]. They cannot deny both because denying [3] involves accepting [2].

Identity-theory physicalists reject [2] and accept [3]. They agree with dualists that something is mental but claim that it is also physical. They identify everything mental with something physical.

Eliminative physicalists accept [2] and reject [3]. They agree with dualists that being mental excludes being physical but claim that nothing is mental. They eliminate the mental.

Dualism is inconsistent with panpsychism, because [2] and [4] together imply that not everything is mental. Thus panpsychists must decide whether to deny [2] or [4]. They cannot deny both because denying [4] involves accepting [2].

Identity-theory panpsychists reject [2] and accept [4]. They agree with dualists that something is physical but claim that it is also mental. They identify everything physical with something mental.

Eliminative panpsychists accept [2] and reject [4]. They agree with dualists that being physical excludes being mental but claim that nothing is physical. They eliminate the physical.

Identity-theory physicalism is consistent with identity-theory panpsychism. The combined view is that everything is both physical and mental.

A weirder theory than either physicalism or dualism is *panpsychism*, which says that everything is *mental*. Two great philosophers soon after Descartes, Baruch Spinoza (1632–77) and Leibniz, held versions of panpsychism. On such a view, even atoms have a primitive form of consciousness. Most philosophers today find panpsychism implausible. Attributing consciousness to an atom seems utterly gratuitous.

Unlike dualism, both physicalism and panpsychism have a unifying category, whether physical or mental. By contrast, dualism splits reality into two separate parts: the physical and the mental. From Descartes on, dualists have struggled to explain how the two parts are connected. In particular, how can mental events cause physical effects, or physical events cause mental effects? For instance, the mental event of a thief at a party deciding to switch off the lights causes her to switch off the lights, and so causes the physical event of the lights going off. That physical event in turn causes the mental event of a guest wondering why the lights went off. For dualists, the mental and the physical are so radically different from each other that everyday interactions between them look inexplicable. Here physicalism and even panpsychism have an advantage, since they place both cause and effect in a single unified world.

Physicalism, dualism, and panpsychism are not the only options. For instance, if numbers and other mathematical objects are *neither* mental *nor* physical, all three theories must be revised.

Philosophers have also developed increasingly sophisticated understandings of 'mental' and 'physical'. I wrote vaguely of mental and physical 'things', but it turns out to matter what kind of thing is in question. It might be a particular event that happened once to someone, like my feeling hot yesterday morning. Alternatively, it might be a general property, which many people have at many times, like the property of feeling hot. Some philosophers are physicalists about particular events but dualists about general properties. For now, we needn't worry about such subtleties and complications. Our aim here isn't to solve the mind–body problem but to see what theoretical disputes in philosophy are like.

Contrary to what Wittgenstein and others thought, few theoretical disputes in philosophy depend essentially on confusion. No doubt various individual physicalists, dualists, and panpsychists are confused in various ways. The terms of their disputes may also need clarification. But even the negative work of clearing up such confusions involves positive theorizing (see Chapter 4). Moreover, we need a positive theory to explain better how knowing, thinking, feeling, deciding, and doing fit into the world as described by natural science. Rival theories for that purpose are on offer. We need a rational basis for choosing between them, or even for rejecting them all. The history of philosophy, including its recent history, indicates that once mere confusions have been cleared up, we are *still* left with rival theories to choose between. There are both unconfused physicalists and unconfused dualists in philosophy today. As in natural science, holding a false theory does not make you confused; it just makes you wrong.

Once the dispute between physicalism, dualism, and panpsychism has been cleared of confusion, why can't we leave natural scientists to settle it? In principle, they can find out exactly what happens in our brains when we think, or feel, or see, or decide. Of course, it is one thing to observe a *correlation* between mental and physical events, and another to postulate an *identity* between the correlated events. But wouldn't it still be good scientific practice to postulate that the mental events *just are* the physical events, if that is the best, most economical way to explain their correlation? Who needs philosophers for that?

If you find the zombie thought experiment convincing, you'll feel that scientists are missing something crucial if they fail to take account of it. Philosophers are the people most trained to apply such thought experiments. But even if zombies are impossible, there are less extreme reasons for not leaving all the work to natural scientists. For we are not asking just about some particular mental events. We are asking about very general *types* of mental event.

One type of mental event is *thinking that 5 + 7 = 12*. There is no law that only humans can think that 5 + 7 = 12. Even if humans are the only creatures on earth to have thought it so far, one day members of future species or sophisticated robots may think it. Inhabitants of other planets may have thought it long ago. Even if humans are the only things in the universe ever to think that 5 + 7 = 12 (which is unlikely), it could have been otherwise. But when robots or radically different lifeforms think that 5 + 7 = 12, what goes on inside them won't look much like what goes on inside us. Their equivalents of brains may differ radically from human brains. Even if scientists can identify in physical terms a general type of event that goes on in human brains when, and only when, their owners think that 5 + 7 = 12, already a big 'if', that type of event is very unlikely to be what goes on in equally physical but non-human thinkers when *they* think that 5 + 7 = 12. Thus we cannot expect such observational and experimental methods to give an adequately general answer to the question "What is it to think that 5 + 7 = 12?" They will not tell us whether the mental *type* of event, thinking that $5 + 7 = 12$, is the same as some physical *type* of event. Questions at that level of generality remain philosophical questions.

This does not mean that observational and experimental methods are simply *irrelevant* to philosophical questions. After all, if a theory is false of human thinking, it is not universally true of all thinking. Moreover, we know far more about human thinking than about any non-human thinking: for us humans, the human case is the natural starting point, though we hope to end up with a much more general theory. To get there, we will need more theoretical methods.

Inference to the best explanation

The methods philosophy needs for choosing between rival theories need not be so different from the more theoretical methods of natural science. We want the theory that best explains whatever evidence we can get. The method of choosing between theories on that basis is called *inference to the best explanation*. It is widely used in both natural science and philosophy (see Figure 5).

Some people find the word 'explanation' too narrow, because they associate it with explaining why some event happened, by identifying its cause: not all theoretical explanations in science do that. For example, Isaac Newton (1643–1727) explained previous laws of terrestrial motion (about objects on earth) and celestial motion (about the planets) by deriving both from more basic laws of motion in general. Basic laws don't *cause* less basic ones, because laws aren't events—laws don't *happen*. Newton explained the less basic laws by unifying them under very simple but informative generalizations. Although most philosophical theories lack the mathematical power and clarity of Newton's laws, they too can be compared with each other by similar criteria, such as simplicity, informativeness, generality, unifying power, and fit with evidence. That general way of choosing between theories is called *abduction*.

5. What best explains these?

Natural science needs abduction because, in principle, many competing theories are logically consistent with all the observational and experimental data available at a given time. Whenever a sensible theory is consistent with such data, so are infinitely many silly theories—for instance, one which says that gravity will behave in accordance with the sensible theory until your next birthday but go haywire after that. All the events we have observed up to now happened *before* your next birthday, so those observations are just as consistent with the haywire theory as with the sensible one, because their predictions diverge only for later events. In that sense, current data cannot distinguish between the two theories. But if scientists had to take all such crazy, pointlessly complicated theories seriously, natural science would grind to a halt. Another example is the theory that the universe was created six minutes ago, complete with apparent memories and fake traces of earlier events, such as dinosaur fossils. In a sense, that theory explains all our data, but it is such a random, arbitrary, unnecessarily complicated hypothesis that it counts as a very bad explanation; it does not deserve to be taken seriously. Similarly, philosophers don't waste time on the random, arbitrary, unnecessarily complicated theory that dualism applies on Sundays but physicalism on other days of the week.

Even when scientists do take two rival theories seriously, they may prefer one on grounds of simplicity. It helps counteract a danger scientists know as *overfitting*. It might seem obvious that we should always prefer a theory that fits the data more closely over one that fits them less closely. But the data usually contain some random errors. In practice, a scientist who always picks equations to fit the data perfectly has to choose very complicated equations to fit what are in fact inaccurate data. As soon as new data become available, they are forced to switch to new, even more complicated equations to fit them too, and so on, reaching no stable conclusion. That's overfitting. A more robust strategy, scientists find, is to prefer simple equations that fit the data more roughly, since doing so makes one less vulnerable to inaccuracies in the data.

Here is a toy example. Imagine a scientist measuring some quantity at one-minute intervals. She comes up with the following sequence of values:

2, 4, 6, 8, 10, 11, 14, 16, 18, 20

It goes up by 2 each time, except around 11. She could take all the numbers at face value, and come up with some complicated hypothesis to fit them. Alternatively, she might guess that she made a mistake in measuring—it should have been 12, not 11—and go with the much simpler hypothesis that really the quantity went up by 2 each time. The former strategy is overfitting; experience shows that it tends to give bad results. The latter strategy is more productive. It is not cheating. Rather, it is taking into account the fallibility of the measurement process.

Overfitting occurs in philosophy too. Philosophers who rely too exclusively on judgements about thought experiments come up with complicated, messy theories to fit all those judgements. They have to keep changing their theories to fit judgements about new thought experiments. Their theories become more and more complicated and messy; they reach no stable conclusion. They make themselves too vulnerable to inaccuracies in their judgements about thought experiments. Even if they are pretty reliable in those judgements, they cannot expect to be *infallible*. Their strategy makes insufficient allowance for occasional errors. If they put more weight on the simplicity of a theory, they would learn to be more critical of their verdicts about thought experiments. Although philosophy needs such verdicts, it also needs a strategy to handle the danger of errors in them. Putting weight on simplicity in comparing theories provides such a strategy.

Chapter 7
Deducing

Deduction in philosophy and elsewhere

Many philosophers are proud to emphasize that they don't
dogmatically assert their views; they *argue* for them. The kind of
argument they often have in mind is *deduction*, in a strictly
logical sense. The conclusion of a deductive argument follows
logically from the premises, its assumptions; to assert the
premises and deny the conclusion would be logically
inconsistent. For instance:

First premise	Either there is no suffering or there is no god.
Second premise	There is suffering.
Conclusion	There is no god.

This argument for atheism is deductively *valid*: *if* the premises
hold, it follows logically that the conclusion holds too. It follows
because the first premise offers two alternatives, of which the
second premise eliminates one, so only the other alternative is left.
This specific form of argument is called *disjunctive syllogism*. It is
one of many deductively valid forms of argument.

Not only philosophers use deduction. Proofs in mathematics are
chains of deductions. Some everyday reasoning too is deductive. If

you reason that your keys are either upstairs or downstairs, and they're not downstairs, so they must be upstairs, you are relying on disjunctive syllogism. According to the ancient Greek philosopher Chrysippus (about 279–206 BCE), even dogs use disjunctive syllogism. One day, when chasing a rabbit, his dog came to a place where the path forked three ways. The dog sniffed at the first two ways, then ran down the third way *without sniffing*. It didn't need to sniff, because it was reasoning "The rabbit went either this, that, or the other way; it didn't go this or that way, so it went the other way".

Since the mid-19th century, deductive logic has progressed in leaps and bounds through the use of precise artificial languages, whose formulas are much clearer in logical structure than sentences of native human languages, like English and Mandarin. Mathematical logic is a branch of mathematics, widely applied in computer science. Indeed, the work of Alan Turing (1912–54)

6. Turing's machine in 1944.

and others in mathematical logic was the basis for the development of the modern computer (see Figure 6). Philosophers often use modern logic to make their arguments more precise and rigorous, sometimes by translating them into an artificial language, where their validity can be checked more easily and reliably. It's like waiting to see what really happened in slow-motion replay, rather than basing one's judgement on the real-time blur of action. But all the power and insight of modern logic ultimately derive from normal human capacities for simple reasoning.

Validity and soundness

In calling an argument valid, one makes no judgement on whether the premises and the conclusion *are* true; one only excludes the case where the premises are true and the conclusion false. A valid argument with true premises, and therefore a true conclusion, is called *sound*. Thus if two arguments have mutually inconsistent conclusions, they can't both be sound, but they can both be valid. Compare the argument at the start of the chapter *for* atheism with an argument *against* atheism, also by disjunctive syllogism:

First premise	Either life has no meaning or there is a god.
Second premise	Life has meaning.
Conclusion	There is a god.

In both displayed arguments, the conclusion really does follow from the premises, so both are valid, but at most one of them is sound: there can't be both a god and no god.

Confronted with two valid arguments for mutually inconsistent conclusions, one must assess their premises. Some premises are obvious truths. For instance, the second premise of the first argument, "There is suffering", is obvious, even if someone somewhere is crazy enough to deny the obvious. But most philosophically significant arguments have at least one non-obvious premise. For instance, the first premises of both displayed arguments are non-obvious. Philosophers then seek further arguments for the non-obvious premises of their original arguments, and then still other arguments for the non-obvious premises of those further arguments, and so on. Where does this regress lead?

An analogy with mathematics may look encouraging. For instance, in arithmetic—the theory of the counting numbers 0, 1, 2, 3,... —one can validly deduce very non-obvious theorems through long proofs from very obvious axioms. Can't one hope to do the same in philosophy? Unfortunately, the history of philosophy suggests not. Although brilliant philosophers have tried that way to determine whether there is a god, all have failed. Experience suggests that the same goes for most other philosophically interesting questions. For instance, physicalism is logically consistent, as is dualism, but they are logically inconsistent with each other, so logic alone cannot settle the dispute between them. In most areas of philosophy, the sort of systematic, deep, general theory to which our understanding most aspires is the least likely to be deducible from obvious premises.

We might lower the standard for our starting premises. We could say: they don't need to be obvious, so long as they are 'intuitive', in some sense. But if we lower the standard enough to obtain valid arguments from premises meeting the new standard to interesting conclusions such as theism or atheism, dualism or physicalism, we may easily find ourselves back as before with pairs of arguments for contrary conclusions. The crucial task will again be to assess the premises; by what arguments are we to do that? In brief, the deductive conception of philosophical method breaks down.

It would be wrong to draw the moral that deduction is unimportant in philosophy. Philosophers rely on it continually. But they do so most successfully in making deductions *from* theories, not *to* theories. For instance, in testing a theory by thought experiment, we draw out its consequences for an imagined scenario, often by deduction. The theory is a universal generalization, an instance of which says something about the case at hand. We saw examples in Chapter 5: from the theory that justified true belief is knowledge, we deduced the consequence that if a man has a justified true belief that there's a fire over there, he *knows* that there's a fire over there. This resembles the scientific method of deducing observable predictions from a theory (plus other assumptions) and then observing whether those predictions are fulfilled. Although natural scientists don't expect to deduce their theories from more or less obvious premises, they still rely heavily on deduction in drawing out the consequences of their theories. Often, the deductions take the form of mathematical calculations.

Deducing consequences from a scientific theory is not just for purposes of prediction. It also plays a key role in *explanation*. For example, explaining why the planets move in elliptical orbits involves deducing such orbits from a theory stating the laws of motion. Philosophical theories have explanatory power too. For instance, some philosophers explain how a mental event can cause a physical event thus: the mental event *is* a physical event, so it's no more problematic than one physical event causing another. They are making a deduction from what is called 'identity-theory physicalism' (see Box 2 in Chapter 6 for details). Explanatory deductions, like predictive ones, often rely on extra background premises, in both philosophy and natural science, but that's no surprise; it's quite consistent with the key role of deduction.

Some theories have low deductive power: little can be deduced from them. This may be for several reasons. A theory may be precise, but hyper-cautious. For instance, a theory saying only "At least one event caused at least one other event" is fairly precise but pretty uninformative. Universal generalizations, of the form "*Everything* is so-and-so", tend to be more informative, since they logically imply an instance about whatever we like: "*This* thing is so-and-so". But even universal generalizations don't tell us much if 'so-and-so' is too vague. Imagine a philosopher who announces, "Everything is a synthesis of being and becoming" and just waffles when asked what 'synthesis of being and becoming' means. The theory may sound impressive at first hearing, but it doesn't tell us much; it's too unclear what its consequences are meant to be. Such uninformative theories have low explanatory power: they explain little. More generally, they don't answer our questions. Precise universal generalizations tend to have more deductive and explanatory power.

Precision-loving philosophers are sometimes criticized for excessive caution, even for intellectual cowardice. The idea is that the truly bold philosophers are those ready to plunge into the depths of obscurity, risking all in murky darkness, while the precision-lovers play trivial games in the clear shallows. It's a nice picture, the vagueness-lovers' safe dream of danger. Wild and woolly prose may sound radical, but it's really the easy, comfortable option, because its unclarity makes it unrefutable. It makes one's mistakes impossible to pin down. The risky option is saying something clear and specific enough to be refuted.

A theory can also have *too much* deductive power, in the extreme case where it is logically inconsistent. In standard logic, an inconsistent theory collapses, because it implies every statement whatsoever, since it cannot consistently deny anything (thus "The moon is and is not made of green cheese" implies "You are the Pope"). In seeming to explain everything, an inconsistent theory explains nothing. Since clarity magnifies deductive power, clear theories are more at risk of this ultimate disaster than unclear ones. They earn correspondingly more credit if they manage to avoid it.

Abduction in logic and mathematics

Given what's been said so far, the role of deduction in philosophy looks very similar to its role in natural science. This may suggest that philosophy is methodologically closer to natural science than to mathematics, where every theorem must have a deductive proof. But that conclusion is premature. For even in mathematics, every proof depends on first principles, which are accepted without appeal to a further proof of them. If you trace a mathematical proof back from its conclusion, step by step, you must eventually come to first principles in a finite number of steps, otherwise it would be circular or go back in an infinite regress, and so be no genuine proof. Thus mathematical proof depends on something non-deductive, the support for its first principles.

What are the first principles in mathematical proof? Some are principles of deductive logic, used in non-mathematical as well as mathematical reasoning, such as the principle that a universal generalization implies any of its individual instances. Others are specifically mathematical principles, such as the *axiom of infinity*, which says that there is an infinite set, one with infinitely many members $(0, 1, 2, 3, \ldots)$.

Some philosophers have tried to dismiss the first principles of logic and mathematics as mere verbal conventions, partial definitions of logical and mathematical words such as 'every' and 'set'. However, those attempts misrepresent the use of such words. For example, the axiom of infinity is not a partial definition of the word 'set'. *Finitists* deny the axiom and hold all sets to be finite. In doing so, they need not misunderstand the word 'set' or advocate a change in its meaning; they may simply think that the axiom (with its current meaning) is false. Like most mathematicians, I take the axiom to be true, but it would be totalitarian to insist that no one *really* disagrees, a sort of 'repressive tolerance'. Human languages leave far more room for diversity of opinion than that. Genuine questions of truth and falsity arise for fundamental principles of logic and mathematics, just as they do for fundamental principles of physics. Those questions should be fairly addressed, not evaded.

What warrants us in accepting some principles of logic and mathematics while rejecting others? They are not all obvious or self-evident. In particular, it is not obvious or self-evident that there is an infinite set. A more promising alternative is to apply the same abductive methodology to the assessment of fundamental theories in logic and mathematics that Chapter 6 applied to theories in natural science and philosophy—a kind of inference to the best explanation. Bertrand Russell took this view. In an essay of 1907, he wrote (using the term 'induction' rather than 'abduction') about the first principles of logic and mathematics, after he had spent years trying to identify them:

> We tend to believe the premises because we can see that their consequences are true, instead of believing the consequences because we know the premises to be true. But the inferring of premises from consequences is the essence of induction; thus the method in investigating the principles of mathematics is really an inductive method, and is substantially the same as the method of discovering in any other science.

Thus we accept the axiom of infinity because we need it to unify mathematics by deriving many already accepted mathematical theories from one new and more fundamental logico-mathematical theory. Russell's description, based on his own experience, fits the historical development of fundamental theories in logic and mathematics far better than does any talk of verbal conventions or apparent self-evidence.

Most research in logic and mathematics is non-fundamental. One proves theorems deductively, applying accepted principles and methods, taking their correctness for granted without asking where they come from. But when their correctness is questioned, the answer is abductive. Thus it is a false contrast to describe natural science and philosophy as abductive, logic and mathematics as deductive. Abduction plays a discreet but fundamental role in logic and mathematics too. We might picture philosophy as somewhere 'between' mathematics and natural science, except that doing so misleadingly suggests a one-dimensional comparison. In respect of abduction, philosophy is closer to natural science than to the non-natural science of mathematics. In respect of real-life experimentation, philosophy is closer to mathematics than to natural science.

Abduction's fundamental role in logic and mathematics shows that real-life experimentation is inessential to abductive methodology as such, even though it is essential to the success of many specific abductive projects. This is a warning not to take abduction's fundamental role in philosophy as a reason to assimilate philosophy to natural science. As a systematic, methodical form of inquiry, philosophy is a science but not a natural science.

Non-neutral logic

When philosophers argue deductively, they usually apply accepted principles and methods of logic and perhaps mathematics, taking their correctness for granted without asking where they come from. This can encourage the impression that logic is a neutral umpire between philosophical theories, without philosophical commitments of its own.

The impression is false. All first principles of logic ever proposed have been challenged on philosophical grounds. The challenges may be mistaken, but they are not *crazy*. In no interesting sense are first principles philosophically neutral *in general*, although they may be accepted by both sides in many particular philosophical disputes.

The most famously contested logical principle is the *law of excluded middle* (LEM), a central principle of classical (standard) logic. Each instance of LEM says that something is either so or not so. That includes statements about the past and future as well as the present. Here is one instance of LEM:

Either you sneeze tomorrow or you do not sneeze tomorrow.

Some philosophers would reject that statement because they regard the future as still unsettled. For them, it's open whether you sneeze tomorrow or not; it could go either way. They argue: "You sneeze tomorrow" isn't yet true or false; "You do not sneeze tomorrow" is also not yet true or false; therefore, the whole "Either … or …" statement itself is not yet true or false. Thus they reject LEM, and with it classical logic. One can pick holes in their reasoning, but it's not crazy.

Traditionally, the worst sin against rationality was to assert a contradiction: you can't have a rational discussion with people who willingly contradict themselves. But some logical paradoxes going back to ancient Greece make it very hard to avoid contradicting oneself. For example, Epimenides the Cretan makes just the following statement (call it 'S'):

This statement is not true.

Is S true? If S is not true, then, since that is what S says, S is true. If S is true, then, by what S says, S is not true. Either way, we get a contradiction, which most logicians do their utmost to avoid. But a few, such as Graham Priest, so-called *dialetheists*, argue that in these paradoxical cases the best option is to embrace the contradiction, asserting:

S is both true and not true.

I am no dialetheist, but I know from experience that you *can* have a rational discussion with Graham Priest. To argue for dialetheism, he even uses the abductive methodology advocated here.

In classical logic, a contradiction logically implies all statements whatsoever (see the end of the section 'Abduction in Logic and Mathematics'). It would be crazy to commit oneself to all statements whatsoever, but dialetheists do not want to go that far. To avoid it, they revise classical logic to enable them to localize the effects of a contradiction, so that most statements *don't* follow from it. The way they do so requires them to reject disjunctive syllogism. Thus they will regard the earlier arguments by disjunctive syllogism for and against atheism as logically invalid, even if they are not the type of example where they think the principle leads one badly astray.

Arguably, dialetheists underestimate the costs of abandoning classical logic. Since classical logic is tacitly used throughout science, restricting it has massive knock-on effects. Dialetheists hope to recover classical logic whenever they need it in non-paradoxical situations, on a case-by-case basis, by adding extra assumptions to the effect, "Classical logic is OK in this case". Those assumptions must be added to all sorts of completely normal scientific explanations in non-paradoxical situations to make them work without granting the general validity of classical logic. Messing up elegant scientific explanations with numerous extra assumptions made up as one goes along reduces the power of those explanations all over science. If instead one retains classical logic and makes adjustments elsewhere, one can avoid such widespread losses of explanatory power, and so strike a better bargain, in terms of the scientific methodology for comparing theories sketched in Chapter 6. Nevertheless, weighing the costs and benefits of rival solutions to the paradoxes is delicate. Dialetheists may have got it wrong, but not *crazily* wrong.

One of the most trivial-sounding principles of logic, with the grand-sounding title 'the reflexivity of identity' (RI), just says that everything is itself. Even RI has been denied. Some philosophers think *nothing* is self-identical, for everything is always changing and, when things change, they are not themselves. Their argument rests on subtle, non-crazy mistakes about how the logic of identity and the logic of time interact, but the result is still that they deny RI.

Developments in natural science have also been taken to motivate revisions of classical logic. Hilary Putnam and a few other non-crazy philosophers argued that the best way to understand some puzzling phenomena in quantum mechanics is by supposing that logic in the quantum world is non-classical. According to the classical principle of *distributivity*, statement (1) below logically implies statement (2), where F, G, and H are three properties a physical system can have:

(1)   The system has F and either G or H.
(2)   The system has either F and G or F and H.

In 'quantum logic', statement (1) does not logically imply statement (2); distributivity fails. This challenge to classical logic is not absurd, and it flouts no linguistic convention. The question is whether loosening distributivity really does help explain what is physically going on in the quantum world. Unfortunately for quantum logic, the answer seems to be "No": it does not solve the underlying problems in physics. Putnam later abandoned quantum logic. The point is that his challenge couldn't simply be dismissed. The intellectually responsible way of meeting it was to think through in detail whether a change of logic would help us understand the quantum world.

Logic and philosophy

As Bertrand Russell wrote, "logic is concerned with the real world just as truly as zoology, though with its more abstract and general features". He wasn't viewing the real world from an ivory tower—he wrote those words in prison during World War I, sentenced to six months for prejudicing Britain's relations with the USA, its ally, by suggesting in a magazine article that American troops in Britain might be used for strike-breaking.

Classical logic is a good theory of the most abstract and general features of the real world. It has no transcendental justification, no proof that ultimately no challenge to it makes sense. It needs no such justification. Rather, classical logic is justified like other scientific theories, by the sort of abductive comparison with its rivals sketched in Chapter 6. Classical logic is simple and elegant. It is logically stronger than most of its rivals: more informative, with more power to unify and explain general patterns. It has been tested far more intensely than any non-classical logic, and found adequate, since it has been the background logic of mathematics and other sciences for millennia. Attempts to show that it doesn't fit the evidence have never succeeded. It is one of our best scientific theories.

Classical logic is also a contribution to philosophy. The abstract and general patterns in reality it describes are of central philosophical significance. They are both of interest in their own right and of value as constraints on philosophical theorizing. Otherwise, it's too easy for philosophers to blame their inconsistencies on classical logic; there's an old saying: "A bad workman blames his tools". Classical logic often forces us to go deeper to solve a problem.

Classical logic concerns the logic of 'not', 'and', 'or', 'every', 'some', and 'is'. Rather than revising classical logic, some logical theories *extend* it. An example is *modal logic*, which concerns the logic of 'can' and 'must', or 'possible' and 'necessary'. For instance, if you *can* sit, it logically follows that either you can sit and sing or you can sit and not sing. By contrast, if you *must* sit, it does not logically follow that either you must sit and sing or you must sit and not sing—singing may be up to you. Modal logic systematically studies which such arguments are valid, which invalid. Since it often matters philosophically whether something is possible or impossible, necessary or contingent, modal logic is the relevant branch of logic for many philosophical arguments (see Figure 7).

Here is an example of a controversial hypothesis in what is called *quantified modal logic*:

Everything is necessarily something.

This implies that you are necessarily something; you couldn't have been nothing. But what if your parents had never met? Would you have been nothing then? If you deny the hypothesis, you are in effect making another statement in the language of modal logic:

Not everything is necessarily something.

Philosophers are currently working out the consequences of each alternative, to see which gives the better overall theory.

Despite the controversies, logic makes obvious progress. Much of that progress is progress in philosophy.

7. Four pioneers of quantified modal logic: clockwise from top left,
Avicenna (Ibn Sina, 980–1037); Rudolf Carnap (1891–1970); Saul
Kripke (1940–); Ruth Barcan Marcus (1921–2012).

Chapter 8
Using the history of philosophy

Is philosophy history?

If you enter a university department of philosophy, you soon find that much—in some places, most—of what's taught there is *history* of philosophy. By contrast, little or none of what's taught in a department of mathematics or natural science is history of mathematics or of natural science. Occasionally, names of mathematicians or scientists are attached to discoveries, but students aren't expected to know how they came to make them, still less to read their original writings, in which those results may be unrecognizable, so alien are the outlook and language. Meanwhile, philosophy students have to read books, or large chunks of them, by long-dead great philosophers, at least in translation. Philosophy seems to have a different relation to its past from that of mathematics and natural science to their pasts.

Few philosophers are happy to leave the history of philosophy to history departments. When past philosophers are studied there, it's called 'history of ideas'. More attention is paid to their lives, their social, political, religious, and cultural contexts and constraints, the circumstances in which they developed, wrote, and taught, what they read and who influenced them, what they took for granted and what they were reacting against, who they were writing for, what contemporary effects their works were intended to have or actually did have, and so on. When the same philosophers are studied in philosophy departments, it's called 'history of philosophy'. The main focus is on what is in their work itself rather than its interconnections with its surroundings at the time. The aim is to understand the content as a living, coherent system of thought that still makes sense to us today.

The history of philosophy is part of philosophy. Still, there is a distinction between putting forward a theory as what some philosopher held and putting it forward as *true*. Scholarly historians of philosophy are usually clear about the difference: they are asking what theory the philosopher held, not what theory is true. Unfortunately, there is another widespread kind of philosophical writing that blurs the line. Some overwhelming thinkers, such as the great German philosopher Immanuel Kant (1724–1804), are often written about like that. When you read, "We cannot know things in themselves", it is left unclear whether the writer is just claiming that *Kant thought that* we cannot know things in themselves, or is actually endorsing Kant's view by claiming in their own voice that we cannot know things in themselves. Confusing the two claims is defensively convenient, for it enables the author to dismiss criticisms aimed at the first claim as missing the point of the second, and criticisms aimed at the second claim as missing the point of the first. If you argue that it's wrong as history, the response is to talk about things in themselves. If instead you argue that it's wrong as philosophy, the response is to talk about Kant. Often, such writing is neither good history nor good philosophy.

On one view, philosophy just *is* the history of philosophy, because there is nothing else for it to be. That view has been very influential, especially in continental Europe, though it is now losing ground. A friend of mine, an Italian philosopher, first visited Oxford University in the late 1970s. She found it charmingly naive that people there were still trying to *solve* philosophical problems. She had been educated, she explained, in a philosophical culture which took for granted that fundamentally different systems have no common ground on which to base a decision between them. On that view, we cannot meaningfully ask which of them is objectively true; we can only think within one historically given system or another, even if we are trying to subvert it from within. I am sometimes asked which philosopher I work on, as though that is what any philosopher must do. I reply Oxford-style: I work on philosophical problems, not on philosophers.

The idea that philosophy can only be the history of philosophy is self-defeating, for it is itself a controversial philosophical option, which we are under no obligation to accept. It is not supported by evidence. Hardly any of the philosophers studied in the history of philosophy, such as those mentioned in this book, themselves wrote on the history of philosophy. Their objective was not to interpret other philosophers' theories, or even their own, but to construct such theories in the first place, for instance about the mind and its place in nature, not radically different from scientific theories. The same applies to most of the theories being developed in philosophy today. Moreover, as already seen, there are ways of deciding rationally between such theories. Identifying philosophy with the history of philosophy is a deeply unhistorical attitude, because it is unfaithful to that history itself. Although studying the history of a philosophical problem (such as free will) is one way of studying that problem, many ways of studying the problem are not ways of studying its history, just as studying a problem in mathematics or natural science is typically not studying its history. Fortunately, the history of philosophy can be and is studied with no imperialist ambition for it to take over the whole of philosophy.

Monuments and influence

One can explore the history of philosophy as a sort of intellectual tourist. Just as an atheist can wander in admiration and awe through a great temple, cathedral, or mosque, so one can read great monuments of philosophy while rejecting the theories they express. Some works, such as Plato's dialogues, are unforgettable masterpieces of literature with obviously artistic qualities of prose style, imagery, and dramatic form. Others, such as Kant's *Critique of Pure Reason* (1781) and Georg Wilhelm Friedrich Hegel's *Phenomenology of Spirit* (1807), are turgidly written but still constitute tremendous works of art by their towering, intricate architecture of ideas.

Of course, even if a building is breathtaking at first sight, the less one understands about its structure and function and how they correspond—for instance, how a temple's spatial layout enabled movements through it to express religious and social meanings—the more superficial is one's appreciation. The same goes for philosophical works. Once one has an intelligent, well-informed guide, one realizes how much one was missing as an ignorant tourist. One learns and values more on every visit. Already at this level, studying the history of philosophy repays the effort.

A great work of philosophy tells a new story about how things are, of a very general, abstract kind. Usually, the author intended the story to be true, but even if it is false, it may still be a good story, and we may enjoy it as such, without illusions. For example, in *Treatise Concerning the Principles of Human Knowledge* (1710) and *Three Dialogues between Hylas and Philonous* (1713), the Irish philosopher-bishop George Berkeley developed the *subjective idealist* view that reality consists of nothing but minds and their ideas, of which trees, tables, and other observable objects are constructs. Cheekily, he argued for his theory as the best defence of common sense and religion against a purely scientific post-Newtonian world view. One might wonder: with friends like Berkeley, who needs enemies? But even if we find subjective idealism an outrage to common sense, we can still enjoy the experience of viewing things through its spectacles, and admire Berkeley's skill in building an elegant and surprisingly robust edifice out of such flimsy immaterial material.

Apart from the intrinsic interest and beauty of philosophical ideas, their history is one key to human history in general. As Berkeley illustrates, much of the battle of ideas between religious and scientific world views has been fought out within philosophy. The word 'idea' itself goes back to Plato. The Austrian philosopher-scientist Ernst Mach (1838–1916) influenced both Robert Musil's novel *The Man Without Qualities* and Albert Einstein's theory of general relativity. Many political arguments are defined in terms of philosophical ideas like *human rights*. Less benignly, the official doctrine of Stalin's Soviet Union was *dialectical materialism*, rooted in 19th-century German philosophy. False theories as well as true ones have effects.

In early 20th-century logic, a question arose that was both mathematical and philosophical: what does it mean to have a 'definite method' for solving a mathematical problem without need of creativity? To answer the question, Alan Turing devised an abstract theory of imaginary *universal computing machines*. Later, in an attempt to break German codes during World War II, he actually built such a machine. Its success helped defeat Nazism. That was the origin of modern computers, which have transformed our world. It is hard, or impossible, to predict in advance what effect a philosophical idea will have on history.

Turing is a reminder that the historical effect of a philosophical theory can depend on its exact content, not just its general tendency. If his theory had been slightly different in detail, it might have been incapable of doing the technical job, and so would not have produced working computers.

Which ideas have influence in philosophy depends on which look convincing or at least promising to other philosophers. Scholars who only think as historians, not as philosophers, may lack the philosophical skills to judge how an idea would have looked to past philosophers. Such historians are not even best placed to judge what ideas a past philosopher was expressing in a given text.

For historical texts are often hard to interpret. Sometimes only part of a manuscript is preserved. Sometimes several versions of a work survive, differing from each other at crucial points. Even without those problems, words and grammar may be multiply ambiguous. Even if the literal meaning is clear, it may be unclear what the author is getting at, how an argument is meant to work, whether a given statement is being endorsed or just set up for later demolition, what moral the reader is expected to draw, and so on. To determine how the text should be read, one must compare various alternative interpretations, to see which makes the most sense. An interpretation that makes the text internally inconsistent is less likely to be what the author intended. Judging the internal coherence of a sophisticated philosophical text requires philosophical skills which those who think as historians rather than philosophers may lack. That is why historians of philosophy must be capable of thinking as philosophers, though they must also be capable of thinking as historians. If you don't know that the Roman Catholic Church had the Italian philosopher-scientist Giordano Bruno burnt at the stake in February 1600 for heresy, you can't consider how that event may have influenced what 17th-century philosophers wrote or didn't write.

Can the history of philosophy help solve philosophical problems?

Suppose that you are interested in contemporary philosophical problems. Will your ability to make progress with them be impeded if you ignore past philosophy?

If you really ignore *all* past philosophy, that includes the past thirty years. You would be trying to redo philosophy from scratch. That would be no more sensible than trying to redo mathematics or physics from scratch, ignoring all previous discoveries. With luck, you would reinvent the wheel. Alternatively, you might invent the square wheel. That's no reflection on you personally.

In all these areas, we have reached where we are now through the combined efforts of hundreds of brilliant thinkers over thousands of years. No one individual human could achieve in a lifetime what they achieved together. There is a myth of the lone genius, thinking everything out for themselves in glorious isolation. That is not how philosophy or mathematics or natural science works. Although much has been achieved there by solitary thought, it was done by thinkers who had already learned much from the work of others. Perhaps the closest to a counterexample was the Indian mathematical genius Srinivasa Ramanujan (1887–1920), but even he started from textbooks. Still less do good philosophers appear like gurus from the wilderness. Philosophy advances by rationally comparing rival ideas, through dialogue, not monologue. One must be involved in the conversation to know which ideas have been proposed as rivals to one's own, and what common ground one has with their proponents to start from in arguing against them. The lone guru lacks such knowledge. Two gurus must learn to listen as well as talk to each other.

In practice, those who make significant original contributions to philosophy are well acquainted with the recent work of other philosophers. To that extent, philosophy resembles mathematics and natural science. The controversial issue is whether philosophers need much more knowledge of the less recent history of their subject than mathematicians and natural scientists need of theirs. Has contemporary philosophy already absorbed all the significant insights of earlier work?

One point is this. It's hard to know what assumptions present philosophy takes for granted until one encounters past philosophy that did *not* take them for granted. That's part of the value of taking them for granted: in order not to waste time thinking about them. But philosophers typically want to detect their assumptions, not let them fly under the radar. "The unexamined life is not worth living," said Socrates, according to Plato. Examining one's life involves identifying what one has been taking for granted. For instance, many contemporary philosophers assume that moral duties always outweigh aesthetic considerations of beauty and ugliness, unaware that they are making a substantive assumption. Reading Friedrich Nietzsche could alert them to alternatives, and perhaps make them question their assumption. Of course, not only reading past philosophy can have that effect. If they moved to Italy (as Nietzsche did), they might understand how that low view of aesthetic values can look less compelling than it does in north-west Europe and North America, cultures heavily influenced by Protestantism. But studying the history of philosophy is one good way of achieving that kind of culture shock.

Once we recognize our assumption, we may reject it as false or unwarranted—sometimes a liberating experience, sometimes a scary one. But we may instead continue to accept it, now consciously. We may try to give it further support. From the history of philosophy, we may learn where it comes from. It's good to know one's intellectual ancestry.

At any time, only a limited range of ideas are under discussion in philosophy. Knowing more of its history expands one's resources. Like good mathematicians, good philosophers have lots of different examples and strategies up their sleeve, to use as needed. The history of philosophy is a prime source for such examples and strategies.

The historical record serves another purpose too. Most philosophical ideas start vague. They can be developed and sharpened in many different ways. The test of an idea is whether *at least one* such version works. If so, the idea is good: that other versions of it don't work doesn't matter. We shouldn't rely on *opponents* of the original idea to find the best version of it. They want it to fail, and so are likely to give up too easily. It's up to the idea's *supporters* to find its best versions. If the most intelligent and ingenious of them struggled for many years to make it work, and still failed, that's excellent evidence against the idea. It's stronger than any one precise argument, for the latter will refute some versions of the idea but not others.

An example is the *verification principle*, advocated by so-called *logical positivists* like Rudolf Carnap from the 1920s onwards. The rough idea was that to make a meaningful statement about the world you must say something that can be verified or falsified by observation. The intention was to include scientific statements while excluding unscientific ones. Logical positivists made numerous clever attempts to find a precise version of the verification principle. All failed, because they turned out either to include obviously unscientific statements or to exclude obviously scientific ones, from the logical positivists' own perspective. That track record of failure is a more powerful argument against the very idea of the verification principle than the individual refutation of any specific version. If there were a workable version of the verification principle, the logical positivists would have found it. Although convoluted attempts to find that holy grail of logical positivism are occasionally still made, they have gone nowhere. To use the helpful terminology of the philosopher of science Imre Lakatos (1922–74), logical positivism is a *degenerating research programme*. The history of philosophy keeps the track record of such efforts. It gives us evidence that an idea is no good, because attempts to make it work led to a degenerating research programme.

In modern times, few philosophical developments have been directly inspired by much earlier work. Even when the older precedents were clear in retrospect, the new ideas often had to be discovered independently before the similarity could be recognized.

For example, the idea of a *possible world*—a fully detailed course of events the universe could have taken—has turned out to be central, technically and philosophically, to understanding the meaning and logic of modal verbs such as 'can' and 'must', 'may' and 'ought'. What's possible is what holds in *some* possible world; what's necessary is what holds in *every* possible world. In the actual world, you are reading this book; in another possible world, this book was never written. Three hundred years ago, Leibniz already wrote about possible worlds. Unlike modern philosophers, he conceived them as ideas in the mind of God, who chose which one to actualize. God chose this one because it is the best of all possible worlds, Leibniz implausibly claimed. But he did not inspire modal logic, which had to develop in its own way, until in the 1940s Carnap found a key technical role for what he called 'state descriptions', not ideas in the mind of God but consistent and complete stories in words. He then remarked that his state descriptions were analogous to Leibniz's possible worlds. Without the independent development of modal logic, the utility of possible worlds would have been unappreciated.

Philosophy is not very different from other disciplines in how its history helps generate new ideas. Still, the history is used more than in mathematics and natural science. Why?

Perhaps more than any other discipline, philosophy is willing to question its own assumptions, as well as those of others. When mathematicians question basic mathematical assumptions, or physicists question basic physical assumptions, they tend to be reclassified as philosophers. But when philosophers question basic philosophical assumptions, they still count as philosophers. Since they keep returning to basics, they have more in common with their distant predecessors: hence a role for the history of philosophy.

Of course, progress in mathematics and natural science often depends on *not* questioning basic assumptions, but instead building on them. Such activity is 'normal science', in the words of the physicist, historian, and philosopher of science Thomas Kuhn (1922–96). Only when normal science hits a crisis is there a return to basics, and a questioning of them, often followed by a scientific revolution, according to Kuhn. Much contemporary philosophy is 'normal philosophy', building on assumptions without questioning them; then the history of philosophy plays only a minor role. However, philosophy also includes more revolutionary or would-be revolutionary activity than most disciplines do, because its traditional intellectual values so encourage and reward the questioning of basic assumptions. The history of philosophy plays a correspondingly larger role.

Surely it is good for our culture to have a discipline as ready to question basic assumptions as philosophy is. But one that routinely questions every assumption will do no more good than children who ask "Why?" whatever they are told. We cannot expect explanations and justifications to go on forever. Putting *all* one's assumptions on hold just means intellectual paralysis. We need knowledge to guide our questioning and determine our priorities. Philosophy must achieve a delicate balance between questioning assumptions and putting them to work. The abductive method, described in Chapter 7, helps achieve that balance.

Chapter 9
Using other fields

Philosophy is one amongst many fields of systematic inquiry: mathematics, physics, biology, history, economics, psychology, linguistics, social anthropology, computer science...none is soundproofed from the rest. Each learns from others. Creativity often involves combining ideas and knowledge from different areas. Philosophy is no exception. That doesn't make it somehow secondary, any more than physics is secondary because it relies on mathematics. If philosophers brought no distinctive skills of their own to encounters with another field, they would add nothing new to its work. Often, the influence goes in both directions, teaching and learning. This chapter illustrates some of the many ways philosophy learns from elsewhere.

History

Philosophy overlaps history, since both include the history of philosophy (see Chapter 8). But other parts of philosophy can also learn from other parts of history.

An example is political philosophy. It asks how society *should* be organized. Some people say the best form of government is benevolent dictatorship. That's a simple theory in political philosophy. Is it true? Benevolent dictatorship is not really a *form* of government, for benevolence isn't a structural matter, it's just a psychological trait someone may happen to have: what ensures that the next dictator will be benevolent? And how does he or she know what people really want or need? Moreover, how does benevolent dictatorship work in practice? That's a question about *history*.

The answer, "It doesn't work in practice, but it's still the best theory" is dodgy. The *point* of a system of government is to work in practice, with living people in real time. When someone advocates such a system, we should demand evidence that in practice it works better than the alternatives. As an example of real-life benevolent dictatorship, people sometimes give Josip Broz Tito (1892–1980), the communist leader of Yugoslavia from 1944 until his death. A few years later, the country broke up in a bloody civil war. Should he be blamed for it, or praised for preventing it happening earlier? What was life like under his rule? How benevolent was he really? I'm hardly neutral, since my father-in-law spent fourteen months in prison for publishing an article abroad criticizing Tito. In any case, assessing Tito's rule is a complex task, requiring deep historical knowledge. If advocates of benevolent dictatorship deny he was an example, they should tell us who was. Then we can assess their alternative examples, in ways properly informed by history. If they say *no* dictator has ever been benevolent, we should ask them how they know that benevolent dictatorship *would* work well if it were tried.

Political philosophers usually discuss much less simple-minded proposals for the best system of government than benevolent dictatorship, like western-style liberal democracy. We should ask similar questions about those proposals too.

History is our only record of how systems of government work in practice, the closest we can get to *experiments* in politics under realistic conditions. To ignore history in deciding the best system is intellectually and politically irresponsible. Although many contemporary political philosophers avoid discussing historical examples in detail, their views still interact with their impressions of history, such as the comparative effects of democracy and dictatorship. The leading American political philosopher John Rawls (1921–2002) divided political philosophy into *ideal theory*, which abstracts away from the darker aspects of real life, such as criminality, corruption, bigotry, and famine, and *non-ideal theory*, which takes them into account. Non-ideal theorists pay more attention than ideal theorists to history. Rawls gave priority to ideal theory, but there is now a move towards non-ideal theory. History may play an increasingly important role in political philosophy over the coming decades. If it is to act as a proper reality check on philosophers' theorizing, rather than just fuel to their prejudices, there will need to be a culture of using history written by serious historians, rather than whatever popular history happens to suit one.

Social anthropology

Social anthropology studies diverse human societies and cultures: how they are organized; what people in them believe, value, make, and do; how they think, feel, and behave. As far as possible, a social anthropologist studies another society from within, living in it, perhaps for years, observing life day by day, learning the language, asking questions. Despite the contrast in method between history and anthropology, both help us understand how other societies, past or present, are in some ways very different from ours, in others very similar. We learn to see another society from within, and our own from outside.

The British anthropologist Edward Evans-Pritchard (1902–73) studied the role of magic for the Azande of central Africa, their belief in witchcraft and their use of oracles to make decisions, by watching the effect of poison on a chicken. Unlike a historian studying the dead, Evans-Pritchard discussed all this with the Azande, raising objections to their beliefs and listening to their replies. A Christian educated under the colonial power, he tried making decisions by poison oracle and found the method workable. He and the Azande engaged in rational human communication about the very things on which they differed so much (see Figure 8).

Some philosophers deny the possibility of communication between different 'conceptual schemes', which they liken to mutually untranslatable languages. Others deny the very possibility of different conceptual schemes. Social anthropology demonstrates the limits of both views. Radical disagreement between human cultures is possible, but so is rational communication across such disagreements. Contrary to what some have thought, languages are not world views or forms of life; they do not dictate how you must think or behave. Instead, languages are more like market-places where people with clashing world views and forms of life can sometimes peacefully exchange ideas.

None of this means that no world view or belief system is truer than another. The extreme relativist belief that all beliefs are somehow equally true implies a refusal to take the challenge of other beliefs seriously. In dismissing the possibility that we are right and they are wrong, it also dismisses the possibility that they are right and we are wrong.

Linguistics

Philosophy is done almost entirely in words. An occasional diagram may help, and some say (in words!) that wordless music, dance, painting, or sculpture can express philosophical ideas, but to discuss the value of those ideas properly we must use words. Language is the essential medium of philosophy. If we misunderstand how words work, we are liable to do philosophy badly.

In assessing philosophical arguments, we look for valid patterns in the words. Is the remark, "What happens must happen" deep or shallow, controversial or trivial? It depends on how the word 'must' is working.

8. Colonial scene: Evans-Pritchard with Zande boys.

Another case: If someone says, "Jane believes that 5 and 7 make 12", one might reasonably object, "She doesn't *believe* they make 12, she *knows* they do". From such examples, some philosophers conclude that there can be knowledge without belief. But wait: if someone says, "Paris is a city in France", one might reasonably object, "It isn't *a city* in France, it's *the capital*", but it would be perverse to conclude that Paris *isn't* a city in France. The point of the objection to "Paris is a city in France" is that it said *too little*, not that it said *too much*. Although it's true as far as it goes, it would have been more helpful, less misleading, to say, "Paris is the capital of France". Similarly, the point of the objection to "Jane believes that 5 and 7 make 12" is that it said too little, not that it said too much. Although it's true as far as it goes, it would have been more helpful, less misleading, to say, "Jane knows that 5 and 7 make 12". The negation in 'doesn't' and 'isn't' is being used as what linguists call *metalinguistic negation*, to reject the previous utterance as inappropriate rather than false. Thus the argument for knowledge without belief depended on neglecting a phenomenon studied by linguists.

Although most philosophical questions can't be answered *just* by understanding how language works, such understanding often enables us to recognize mistakes in arguments for bad answers to them. Since linguistics studies how language works, familiarity with it helps to avoid philosophical errors.

One branch of philosophy, philosophy of language, studies language in its own right. It engages closely with linguistics, especially semantics, which concerns linguistic meaning, and pragmatics, which concerns the use of language in various conversational contexts. Philosophy of language and linguistics overlap extensively. Indeed, much of the theoretical framework for contemporary semantics and pragmatics was devised by philosophers of language. They include Donald Davidson, Richard Montague, David Kaplan, Saul Kripke, David Lewis, and Hans Kamp in semantics, and J.L. Austin, Paul Grice, and John Searle in pragmatics. Their research programmes have been applied and developed by linguists, often using similar methods but on more languages and with a broader range of evidence. Philosophers have always been interested in language, the dominant human means of expressing ideas and communicating information: no wonder they continue to learn from linguistics.

Psychology

Traditionally, it was philosophy that studied the mind. Typically, the method was unsystematic introspection: looking into one's own consciousness and trying to observe what was going on there, then reasoning about the results.

From the 19th century on, more systematic experimental methods were introduced to study and measure mental phenomena such as the intensity of feelings. Psychology became more like a natural science and split from philosophy. Nevertheless, just as contemporary philosophers of language engage closely with linguistics, so contemporary philosophers of mind engage closely with psychology. For instance, if you're interested in the nature of perception—sight, hearing, touch, smell, and taste—or memory, it would be foolish to ignore what experimental psychology has discovered about them. Introspection has proved an unreliable way of finding out what's going on in one's own mind. Even though one seems to have a view from the best seat, most of the action is happening offstage. The focus of one's attention is far narrower than it seems. Philosophy of mind needs experimental psychology to keep it honest and to go deeper.

Both experimental psychologists and philosophers of mind think about perceptual illusions, which reveal unexpected limits to the reliability of the heuristics—rules of thumb—on which we rely to make sense of our perceptions. A famous example is the Müller-Lyer illusion, discovered in 1889. In the usual version, it involves two parallel lines of equal length, one with arrowheads added at each end, the other with fins added at each end (see Figure 9).

The line with fins looks longer than the line with arrowheads. One striking feature of the illusion is that it persists after discovery. Even when one has measured the lines, and knows that they are of

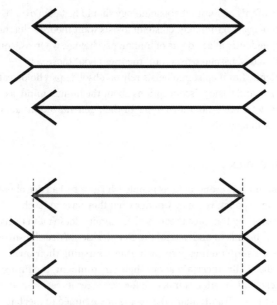

9. The Müller-Lyer illusion.

equal length, one line still *looks* longer than the other. The moral for philosophers is that perceptual *appearances* are not perceptual *beliefs*. What persists is the appearance that one line is longer, not the belief that it is longer.

Philosophy of mind isn't the only branch of philosophy that learns, or should learn, from psychology. Some epistemologists still cling to the view, inspired by Descartes, that fundamentally the only evidence one has to go on is one's own present internal states of consciousness; the justification of all one's other beliefs depends on their relation to that basis. Supposedly, one has direct access to one's internal consciousness, and only indirect access to the external world. That picture makes little sense unless internal consciousness is transparent to some sort of introspection. Such assumptions are hard to reconcile with contemporary psychology.

None of this means that epistemology should be taken over by psychology. Legitimately, epistemologists want theories that hold independently of accidents of human psychology, whereas, equally legitimately, psychologists want theories about those very accidents. But if epistemologists rely on obsolete psychological theories and basic misconceptions about the human mind, as many do, there is not much hope for their generalizations about all possible minds.

Economics

If you think of economists as people who give bad advice about economic policy, you may wonder what they have to teach philosophers. But most theoretical economics doesn't aim to give advice. It aims to understand the complexities of decision-making for agents interacting with each other, pursuing their own agendas while uncertain about their environment, the future, and each other, often competing for scarce resources, sometimes cooperating. Traditionally, the agents are assumed to meet at least minimal standards of rationality: they behave consistently, even if they don't care about any higher good. For instance, if they prefer apples to oranges, and oranges to pears, they don't also prefer pears to apples. Though aware that in practice humans sometimes behave inconsistently, economists treat the assumption of rationality as a good enough approximation to make a helpful starting point. Experimental economics investigates the gap between the predictions of the idealized models and observed human behaviour.

The most theoretical economics is not unlike philosophy in its levels of abstraction and generality, though philosophy tends to be more concerned with questioning basic assumptions, economics with using them as a precise framework within which to develop ever more sophisticated mathematical models. Philosophy and economics overlap extensively in ideas about what makes a decision rational; each can learn from the other.

In many cases of cooperation or competition, what each side does depends on what it predicts the other will do. Thus I am predicting your predictions about my predictions, and you are predicting my predictions about your predictions, and so on, as if to infinity. Our decisions depend on our predictions. If you know that I know that you know where the money is hidden, you may take special precautions to hide your movements from me. If you think that I think that you don't know where it's hidden, you may not bother to take those precautions. Thus complex structures of knowledge of knowledge and beliefs about beliefs can make a practical difference.

Epistemic logic studies such complex knowledge structures. In its modern form, it comes from the work of the Finnish philosopher Jaakko Hintikka (1929–2015), who developed it to cast light on traditional philosophical questions of self-knowledge. If you know something, do you know that you know it? If you *don't* know something, do you know that you don't know it? In my own work, I have studied models of agents who know something even though it's almost certain on their own evidence that they don't know that thing. Economists and computer scientists found that epistemic logic was the best framework for some of their own investigations, and made major theoretical contributions to the field. The strategy is to study mathematical models of the knowledge of agents who are idealized in some ways but limited in others, in order to isolate the specific effects of those limitations. For instance, the agents may be perfect at making logical deductions, but still ignorant of how much other agents know. Some of my own most fruitful collaborative research has been with a theoretical economist, Hyun Song Shin, in epistemic logic.

Decision theory, epistemic logic, and similar inquiries are philosophical in their aims, mathematical in their methods, and spread across many fields, including economics and computer science, in their applications. Although philosophers bring a distinctive emphasis to such collaborations, as they should, their interest in them is not radically different. The boundary between philosophy and non-philosophy runs across a continuous landscape.

Computer science

Theoretical computer scientists got interested in epistemic logic because they were working on *distributed systems*. Such a system distributes its work across several computers, running simultaneously (concurrent processing). Those computers need to communicate with each other. One computer sends a message to another, and needs to 'know' that the message was received. Thus the second computer needs to send a message back to the first, so that the first computer 'knows' that the second computer 'knows' the information in the original message. The second computer may also need to 'know' that the first computer 'knows' that the second computer 'knows' the information, and so on. Epistemic logic is the best framework for a general theory of such issues.

But epistemic logic is not the central connection of computer science to philosophy. Fundamental to computer science is the distinction between *hardware* and *software*. Your laptop, the physical machine that can be dropped on the floor, is hardware. A program that runs on it, the ordered set of instructions, is software. Many different programs can run on the same computer, and the same program can run on many different computers, even of different makes. Software is more abstract than hardware. Philosophers have used that idea to understand the distinction between mind and body. Both you and an intelligent extraterrestrial may know that 5 + 7 = 12, even though its 'brain' is quite different from yours in chemical structure. The hardware is different but this bit of software, the knowledge that 5 + 7 = 12, is the same. You and the extraterrestrial may run the same program for doing arithmetic. Your mind can no more be reduced to your body than software can be reduced to hardware. But that doesn't mean you are partly made of an extra substance, 'soul-stuff', any more than your laptop is partly made of an extra substance, 'program-stuff'.

Some philosophers reject the analogy between mind and software. According to Chalmers, for instance, a zombie can run your software but not your consciousness. Others regard consciousness as just super-sophisticated software. Either way, until we distinguish software from hardware, we have hardly begun to explore the resources available to physicalists for understanding the nature of mind. Moreover, further developments in computer science and artificial intelligence show just how much software can do.

Biology

One central strategy in philosophy of mind is to understand mental states by their *function*. What are knowledge, belief, desire, intention, emotion, sensation *for*? The question suggests one limitation of the software analogy. Normally, a program is for whatever its programmer intended it to be for, but humans aren't programmed in that sense. Of course, our parents and teachers may have intentions for us, and some think Society or God also has intentions for us, but they don't write most of our specific mental states as a programmer writes instructions. We don't even intend most of our own mental states in advance; we just find ourselves in them. For example, when scratched by thorns, you don't *intend* to feel pain; you simply feel it. Nevertheless, it still makes sense to ask what pain is for, and to suggest that its function is to alert us to injury, so that we can act accordingly. Such hypotheses may help explain the nature of mental states.

How can we understand this talk of functions without intentions? The best place to look is biology. The function of a heart is to pump blood round the body, whether anyone intends it to do so or not. After all, most animals with hearts have no idea that hearts pump blood. Nor is biological function a matter of what *usually* happens. The function of sperm is to fertilize eggs, but most sperm never fertilize anything. An evolutionary explanation is more promising. *Very* roughly, there are sperm because past sperm occasionally fertilized eggs. Similarly, perhaps, we feel pain because feeling pain sometimes helped our ancestors protect themselves from injury. At a more general level, mightn't the function of *knowledge* be to enable one to adapt quickly and flexibly to complex changes in one's environment?

Philosophers disagree about how much can be explained in terms of biological functions. But without them, the philosopher's toolbox of instruments of understanding would be significantly poorer.

Physics

Metaphysics is the branch of philosophy that studies the general nature of reality: its structure and content. The name may suggest that metaphysics is about the aspects of reality that physics cannot reach, but that's a misunderstanding. Originally it just meant the book after the *Physics* in the collection of Aristotle's works. Since physics studies the general nature of *physical* reality, its structure and content, its interests overlap those of metaphysics. For example, both physics and metaphysics study *time*.

Some try to distinguish the two concerns with time by claiming that philosophers study the *logic* of time, or our *experience* of time, while physicists study its physical aspects, but no such separation works. Some questions about time belong to both physics and metaphysics. Can time pass without change? Can time end? Between any two instants, is there another instant? Those questions concern the nature of time itself, not just our experience or descriptions of time.

The division of events into past, present, and future is fundamental to everyday thought about time. But Einstein's special theory of relativity makes trouble for that division, since it implies that two events may be simultaneous in one observer's frame of reference yet not in another's. Nothing seems to make one frame 'right', the other 'wrong'. This threatens the usual assumption of a single time order for all events. It remains controversial just how much of the common-sense metaphysics of time special relativity undermines. But a philosopher working on the metaphysics of time without worrying about the implications of Einstein's theory would be far too complacent.

The case of time is not the only example. The interpretation of quantum mechanics is a problem for both philosophers and physicists. Whether to count people as 'philosophers of physics' or 'theoretical physicists working on foundational questions' may depend as much on whether they happen to be employed in a department of philosophy or physics as on what research they do. They may ask similar questions, and use similar methods to answer them.

Mathematics

One way or another, most subjects use numbers, and so rely on mathematics. They classify and count or measure, generating statistical data. Hypotheses are more or less probable; the best framework for reasoning systematically about such matters is the mathematical theory of probability. Once again, philosophy is no exception to the rule. Chapter 10 explains one important role for mathematics in philosophy.

Chapter 10
Model-building

Models in science

Many natural scientists aim at a distinctive kind of progress which philosophers are starting to recognize as an appropriate aim for them too.

The stereotype of scientific progress is discovering a new law of nature. Such laws are meant to be universal generalizations about the natural world, holding without exception for all times and places, by some sort of necessity: nice, if you can find one. However, most natural and social science studies messy complex systems—cells, animals, planets, galaxies, families, organizations, societies—which are hard to characterize by universal laws. What laws must hold for all tigers, for example? "All tigers are striped" won't do, because there are albino tigers. "All tigers are four-legged" won't do either, because there are three-legged tigers, and so on. "All tigers are animals" is true, but doesn't get us far. Although tigers obey the fundamental laws of physics, like everything else in nature, that won't console a biologist who wants to say something specific about living things as contrasted with elementary particles and stars. If we keep watering down our initial attempts, we may eventually reach something exceptionless, but the danger is that it will be too weak and uninformative to be of much interest. This isn't just a problem about animals. Complex systems of all shapes and sizes tend to be messy and unruly.

To manage the problem, scientists have revised their objectives. Instead of seeking universal laws about complex systems, they build simplified *models* of them. Occasionally these are physical models: water running through a sand tray to model a river eroding its banks, a construction of coloured rods and balls to model a DNA molecule. More typically, the models are abstract, defined by mathematical equations which describe how a hypothetical system changes over time. The hypothetical system is vastly simpler than the real-life systems of interest, but still has a few of their key features. The strategy is to analyse the behaviour of the hypothetical system mathematically, in the hope that it will simulate some puzzling aspects of the real-life systems' behaviour, and thereby cast light on them.

For example, you might wonder why a population of predators—say, foxes—and a population of prey—say, rabbits—keep oscillating, though rises and falls in one do not coincide with rises and falls in the other. A key point is that, holding other things equal, the more foxes there are, the more rabbits get eaten, but the more rabbits there are, the more fox cubs survive. One can write down differential equations that express the rate of increase or decrease of each population in terms of the current number of predators and prey. They are known as the Lotka–Volterra model. In most ways, it grossly over-simplifies: it ignores changes in the vegetation the rabbits feed on, changes in the tendency of humans to hunt foxes and rabbits, variations amongst foxes, variations amongst rabbits, and so on. Since such factors make a difference, the equations are not universal laws. Indeed, they couldn't be, since for mathematical reasons the change in population is treated as continuous, even though in real life it changes in whole numbers: when one of 200 rabbits dies, the number goes straight down to 199, with no intermediate time when the number of living rabbits was 199.5. Nevertheless, despite all these oversimplifications, the model correctly predicts some general structural features of population change in predator–prey species. Much progress in natural science is now of this kind. Once we have a successful model, we can try building a little more real-life complexity back into it, step by step, but the models will always be vastly simpler than real life itself—otherwise they would be too complex to analyse.

Sometimes there is no workable alternative to model-building. For example, biologists ask why two-sex reproduction is the norm for animals, since reproduction by three sexes or none is possible in principle. If you want to understand why a phenomenon *doesn't* occur, you can't go out and observe and measure it. Instead, a good strategy is to build hypothetical models of the phenomenon to see how it goes 'wrong'. You might study a model where both two-sex reproduction and three-sex or no-sex reproduction occur, to see which does better, perhaps in achieving genetic variation within the species, which enables it to adapt evolutionarily to changes in the environment. Such models aim not to predict observed quantities but to explain an absence.

Models in philosophy

Humans are a classic example of messy complex systems. In one way or another, much—though not all—of philosophy is about humans. Thus moral and political philosophy mainly concern a good human life and a good human society. Philosophy of science concerns human science; philosophy of art concerns human art; philosophy of language concerns human language. Though philosophy of mind pays some attention to non-human animal minds, its main focus is on human minds, and in any case non-human animals are messy complex systems too. Though in principle epistemology concerns all knowledge, in practice it mainly concerns human knowledge. Logic and metaphysics are partial exceptions, since they tend to deal with matters so basic that messy complexity is less relevant, and informative, precise, exceptionless laws can be formulated. For the rest, however, one might expect a model-building strategy to be appropriate.

That is not how most philosophers have seen it. Many still aim at exceptionless universal laws, even about messy complex systems—humans—for whom natural scientists have mainly abandoned that ambition. In that respect, philosophers have done their field a disservice by inadvertently setting it up for failure, making it search for something that isn't there. People who contrast progress in natural science with deadlock in philosophy often do so on the basis of a false image of each side. Failing to appreciate how much scientific progress consists in building better models, they fail to ask how much philosophical progress consists in building better models too.

We have already seen an example of progressive model-building in philosophy: epistemic logic advances in just that way (Chapter 9). Its models are not universal laws; they involve grossly unrealistic simplifications. Nevertheless, they cast light on human knowledge in the manner of a scientific model.

When philosophers work with probabilities, they typically use models, without emphasizing the fact. For instance, epistemologists often use a lottery as a simple model of uncertainty. To make things definite, suppose that exactly 1,000 tickets have been sold, numbered in order; there's just one winner, chosen at random. Thus if you have one ticket, its probability of losing is 999/1,000. When chance is in play like this, how probable should a statement be for you to believe it? You might decide that requiring 100 per cent certainty is an unreasonably high standard, and resolve to believe whatever has a probability of at least 95 per cent. Immediately, you have a problem. By your rule, you believe that the winning ticket number is at least 51 (since that is 95 per cent probable), and you believe that the winning number is at most 950 (because that too is 95 per cent probable), but you refuse to believe that the winning number is between 51 and 950 inclusive (because that combined statement is only 90 per cent probable). Thus you believe each of two statements separately, but you refuse to put them together, to believe their conjunction. It's like accepting "He's British" and "He's a criminal" but refusing to accept "He's a British criminal" (about the same person). A politician who did that in a TV debate could be made to look very stupid by opponents, at least with voters who cared about consistency. You might think that 95 per cent was a bad choice of threshold for belief, and choose a different threshold instead, for instance 99 per cent, corresponding to the rule, "Believe what is at least 99 per cent probable". But a little calculation shows that the only thresholds for belief which avoid all such lottery problems are 0 per cent and 100 per cent. Since a threshold of 0 per cent means believing every statement whatsoever—total credulity—you are forced back to a threshold of 100 per cent, the standard of certainty you already rejected as unreasonably demanding. Thus even such a 'toy' model can illustrate the difficulties of basing belief on probabilities.

If you think about the lottery model, you can quickly identify some of its simplifying assumptions. For instance, it assumes that you know exactly how many tickets have been sold. In practice, the organization running the lottery may not announce or even know how many tickets have been sold; even if they announce a number, you may give a non-zero probability to the hypothesis that they are mistaken or lying. Then you may also give a non-zero probability to the winning number being 1,001 (since more than 1,000 tickets may have been sold), and you may give a higher probability to the winning number being 1 than to its being 1,000 (since fewer than 1,000 tickets may have been sold). But taking account of all those realistic complications is not time well spent. Thinking about the simple model goes more quickly to the heart of the problem. When more complex probabilistic models are needed to understand more intricate problems, mathematically minded epistemologists construct them too.

In philosophy of language, model-building goes back at least to Carnap. To understand what he was up to, we first need some background in semantics, the theory of meaning.

A striking feature of human languages is that once you master a few words and grammatical constructions, you can use them to build a potential infinity of meaningful sentences, for instance "Picasso slept", "Picasso's aunt slept", "Picasso's aunt's aunt slept", and so on. You can understand them even if you have never heard or read them before. The central project of modern semantics is to explain how the meaning of a complex expression (like one of the quoted sentences) is determined by the meanings of the simpler components of which it is composed (like "Picasso", "aunt", "slept", and the possessive "s"), and how they are put together—"Cats scratch dogs" and "Dogs scratch cats" have different meanings but the same components. Nor is the meaning of a sentence a mere list of the meanings of its component words, since that would make the sentence a mere list of words; such lists do not say anything true or false, unlike sentences. For example, the sentence "Napoleon died in 1815" says something false, while "Napoleon died in 1821" says something true—he did die in 1821. Thus the meanings of words and other expressions must be able to combine with each other, so that sentences can say something true or false. To explain how such combining can work, one needs a clear story about what meanings are. This whole vast project is called *compositional semantics*, to which both philosophers of language and linguists have contributed.

Before Carnap, logicians made considerable progress in compositional semantics by treating the meaning of an expression as its *extension*, its actual application out there in the world. At its simplest, the extension of the name 'Picasso' is the man Picasso himself; the extension of the noun 'cat' is all cats. The extension of a sentence is simply truth or falsity, depending on whether it says something actually true or false. Thus the extension of "Napoleon died in 1815" is falsity while the extension of "Napoleon died in

1821" is truth. *Extensional semantics*, this kind of compositional semantics, explains how the extension of a complex linguistic expression is determined by the extensions of the simpler expressions of which it is composed and how they are combined. The approach turned out to work very nicely for sentences built up using logical words such as 'and', 'or', 'not', 'every', and 'some', which already enable one to build up more and more complex sentences (see Box 3 for some rules of extensional semantics, closely related to the rules for the same words in Chapter 3's Box 1 on logic games).

However, extensional semantics ran into a roadblock with *modal* words, such as 'can' and 'must', or 'possibly' and 'necessarily'. Compositional semantics should apply to them. For example, the meaning of "Possibly Napoleon died in 1815" is composed from the meaning of the word 'possibly' combined with the meaning of the simpler sentence "Napoleon died in 1815". Since extensional semantics equates the meaning of a sentence with its truth-value, it implies that when the meaning of 'possibly' combines with the truth-value of "Napoleon died in 1815" the result is the truth-value of "Possibly Napoleon died in 1815". The truth-value of "Napoleon died in 1815" is falsity, while the truth-value of "Possibly Napoleon died in 1815" (understood in the relevant way) is truth—although he didn't die in 1815, he could have done. Thus extensional semantics implies: *when the meaning of 'possibly' combines with falsity, the result is truth.* But now consider an inconsistent sentence, like "Some dogs are not dogs". The truth-value of "Some dogs are not dogs" is falsity, while the truth-value of "Possibly some dogs are not dogs" is *also* falsity—it couldn't be that some dogs are not dogs. But extensional semantics implies that when the meaning of 'possibly' combines with the truth-value of "Some dogs are not dogs", the result is the truth-value of "Possibly some dogs are not dogs", in other words: *when the meaning of 'possibly' combines with falsity, the result is falsity.* Hence extensional semantics makes inconsistent predictions about the result when the meaning of 'possibly' combines with falsity. For similar reasons, it makes inconsistent predictions about the result when the meaning of 'necessarily' combines with truth.

Carnap realized that extensions carry too little information for the meanings of modal words like 'possibly' and 'necessarily' to work on. The underlying problem is that extensional semantics only considers extensions in the *actual* world, whereas modal words are sensitive to extensions in non-actual but *possible* worlds too (for Carnap's own way of putting it, see Chapter 8). To solve the problem of developing a compositional semantics for modal words like 'possibly', he equated meanings with *intensions* rather than extensions. The intension of a word or sentence is the entire spectrum of its extensions across all possible worlds, actual and non-actual. Carnap showed how the meaning of 'possibly' combines with the intension of any sentence 'A' to give the intension (and extension) of 'Possibly A', and likewise for 'necessarily'. In effect, he interpreted 'possibly' as 'in some possible world' and 'necessarily' as 'in every possible world'. Thus, instead of an extensional semantics, Carnap gave an *intensional semantics* for modal words. He also showed how, wherever extensional semantics works well, it can easily be turned into intensional semantics (if you want a taste of intensional semantics, see Box 3).

Carnap gave a complete intensional semantics for an artificial formal language: every formula, however complex, has an intension, determined step by step from the intensions of the simplest constituents of which it is composed. It is a much more sophisticated model of meaning than extensional semantics. Through the work of Richard Montague, Saul Kripke, David Lewis, and many others, Carnap's intensional semantics has massively influenced both philosophy of language and semantics as a branch of linguistics. Although the models have become still more elaborate, they preserve the crucial move from extensions to intensions.

Carnap worked in a more model-building spirit than his predecessors. He did not construct his formal language to do

Box 3 Extensional and intensional semantics

Extensional Semantics

Complex sentences are built up from simpler ones using 'and', 'or', and 'not'. The extension of a sentence is its truth-value, either truth or falsity. The extension of a complex sentence is determined from the extensions of its component sentences by these rules ('A' and 'B' are any sentences of the language):

and   If 'A' is true and 'B' is true, then 'A and B' is true.
      If 'A' is false or 'B' is false, then 'A and B' is false.

or   If 'A' is true or 'B' is true, then 'A or B' is true.
      If 'A' is false and 'B' is false, then 'A or B' is false.

not   If 'A' is true, then 'Not A' is false.
      If 'A' is false, then 'Not A' is true.

Intensional Semantics

Complex sentences are built up from simpler ones using 'and', 'or', 'not', 'necessarily', and 'possibly'. The intension of a sentence is its spectrum of truth-values over all possible worlds. The intension of a complex sentence is determined from the intensions of its component sentences by these rules ('A' and 'B' are any sentences of the language; w is any possible world):

and   If 'A' is true in w and 'B' is true in w, then 'A and B' is true in w.
      If 'A' is false in w or 'B' is false in w, then 'A and B' is false in w.

or   If 'A' is true in w or 'B' is true in w, then 'A or B' is true in w.
      If 'A' is false in w and 'B' is false in w, then 'A or B' is false in w.

not   If 'A' is true in w, then 'Not A' is false in w.
      If 'A' is false in w, then 'Not A' is true in w.

necessarily	If 'A' is true in every possible world, then 'Necessarily A' is true in w.
	If 'A' is false in some possible world, then 'Necessarily A' is false in w.
possibly	If 'A' is true in some possible world, then 'Possibly A' is true in w.
	If 'A' is false in every possible world, then 'Possibly A' is false in w.

mathematics in or to reveal the hidden essence of all languages. He constructed a simple model language to demonstrate a way for words like 'possibly' and 'necessarily' to work. He thereby cast light on natural languages too. As we learn ever more of the extraordinary complexity underlying even the most ordinary conversations, philosophers of language and linguists will have to rely increasingly on a model-building methodology.

Working models, counterexamples, and error-fragility

Models are fun. You can play with them. That's not just an incidental side benefit; it's what they are for, in both natural science and philosophy. We learn by manipulation, playing about: if you can't manipulate the real thing, a good second-best is often to manipulate a model of it. You can fiddle with this or that component, changing it slightly to see what difference it makes, what varies with what. That way you come to understand more deeply how the model works. If the model is any good, you thereby come to understand better how the real thing works too. For instance, you can't arbitrarily change how English works, to see what difference it makes, but you can arbitrarily change the rules of an artificial language, and calculate the consequences.

To be easily manipulated, a model should be defined in mathematically or logically precise and tractable terms. If the definition is vague, or too complicated, its consequences are unclear: one has to fall back on one's prior philosophical instincts to guess how it behaves, instead of using the model to test those instincts. By contrast, a well-defined model allows one to calculate rigorously how it and variations on it behave, bypassing those prior instincts, and so to learn something unexpected. With a model-building methodology, rigour and playfulness go naturally together.

The rigour of model-building is not the rigour most philosophers are used to. Traditional philosophical rigour requires dismissing a claim once a counterexample to it has been given. In that sense, most models are born refuted, because they involve false simplifying assumptions. For instance, models in epistemic logic typically idealize away from the logical imperfections of normal humans. Some philosophers dismiss those models accordingly.

In physics, models of the solar system may treat a planet as a point mass, as if all its mass were concentrated at its centre. Of course, physicists know that planets are not point masses and do not behave exactly like them. Nevertheless, physicists do not dismiss such models, for they also know that much can be learned from them. By contrast, if one tried to write into the model a fully accurate description of the planet, with all its craters and bumps, the result would be too complicated to permit calculation. It takes skill to distinguish amongst the features of a model those which have lessons to teach us from those which are mere artefacts of the need to keep things simple. Philosophers are having to learn that skill.

To many philosophers, dismissing the true counterexample rather than the false generalization seems like a disregard for truth. It would indeed be intellectually irresponsible to go on *believing* the generalization in the face of a clear counterexample. But that's not the model-building attitude. One can recognize that a generalization is both false and a key component of a model that points us towards genuine truths.

If counterexamples don't refute a model, what does? Within the model-building methodology, what displaces a model is a better model. Part of its superiority may be that it deals more adequately with counterexamples to the old model, but it should also reproduce in its own way the old model's successes. A new model with that combination of virtues may be very hard to find.

Model-building contrasts with the methodology of *conjectures and refutations*, championed by the philosopher of science Karl Popper (1902–94). On the crude version of his view, scientists put forward bold conjectures, informative universal generalizations, which can be falsified but never verified. A single negative instance, a counterexample, will falsify the generalization; no finite number of positive instances will verify it. Scientists do their utmost to refute it by finding such a counterexample. Once it is refuted, they put forward another bold conjecture, and so on.

One problem for such a falsificationist methodology, in both natural science and philosophy, is that it is *error-fragile*. In other words, a single mistake can have disastrous consequences. For suppose that we are testing a bold conjecture, and take ourselves to have found a counterexample. As good falsificationists, we dismiss the conjecture and go on to the next one. But what if the counterexample was a mistake? We are fallible; sometimes we misjudge an instance or two. In that case, the original conjecture may have been true after all. But we never return to it; we are too busy testing new bold conjectures. Philosophers' reliance on counterexamples can be alarmingly close to crude falsificationism: once a counterexample is accepted, there's no going back on it. By contrast, the model-building methodology is much less error-fragile, for it gives no such decisive power to a single judgement. Models are compared over a variety of dimensions.

None of this means that philosophy should go over entirely to a model-building methodology. In some areas, such as logic, we have found many true and informative universal generalizations. In others, good models may be too much to expect. Even where good models are available, as in epistemology, we may do best by using *several* methods. For if each independently pulls in the same direction, that's stronger evidence that it's the right direction. Such a combination of methods is more robust, unless they pull in opposite directions.

The potential of the model-building methodology for philosophy is only beginning to be explored. Its scope and limits should be clearer fifty years from now.

Chapter 11
Conclusion: the future of philosophy

Philosophy is a science in its own right, interconnected with the others and as autonomous as they are. It is also under constant pressure to be something else: lifestyle advice or political polemic, moralizing sermon or grammar lesson, godless religion or unreadable literature, pop physics or pop biology, pop psychology or pop neuroscience, calculation or opinion poll. These pressures are hard to withstand, because they express deep-rooted though conflicting expectations of philosophy and play on philosophers' own insecurities about their field. Most of all, they depend on incomprehension—amongst both philosophers and non-philosophers—of how philosophy could be what it is. I hope that this book will do something to reduce the incomprehension. Whether or not it does, who knows how well philosophy will survive the cultural prejudices against any enterprise of its kind?

Still, philosophy arises from a natural drive in articulate human curiosity to go to one sort of extreme in its questions, and a determination to use the most apt methods available to answer them, no substitutes accepted. That drive and that determination will not easily become extinct.

Progress in philosophical theories makes for progress in philosophical methods, and progress in philosophical methods makes for progress in philosophical theories. Surely the toolbox of methods shown in this book can be improved. Just as other sciences improve their methods, it will happen not by some melodramatic break with the past, but by a difficult iterative process of self-refinement. Perhaps some reader of this book will contribute to that process.

References and further reading

The Oxford Handbook of Philosophical Methodology (Oxford: Oxford University Press, 2016), edited by Herman Cappelen, Tamar Szabó Gendler, and John Hawthorne; *The Palgrave Handbook of Philosophical Methods* (Basingstoke: Palgrave Macmillan, 2015), edited by Chris Daly; and *The Cambridge Companion to Philosophical Methodology* (Cambridge: Cambridge University Press, 2017), edited by Giuseppina D'Oro and Søren Overgaard, are massive collections of essays, primarily aimed at professional philosophers and graduate students in philosophy. Some of the essays address the contrast between two broad traditions in recent philosophy, usually called 'analytic' and 'continental' philosophy. I do not discuss this in this book because each tradition is methodologically too diverse in itself to permit useful discussion in general terms. For what it is worth, this book is written from a recognizably 'analytic' perspective.

The Philosopher's Toolkit: A Compendium of Philosophical Concepts and Methods (Oxford: Wiley-Blackwell, 2nd edition, 2010) by Julian Baggini and Peter Fosl is aimed at a general readership and organized as a work of reference, with many short entries.

Philosophical Devices: Proofs, Probabilities, Possibilities, and Sets (Oxford: Oxford University Press, 2012) by David Papineau explains the logical and mathematical tools used by technically minded philosophers.

The Philosophy of Philosophy (Oxford: Wiley-Blackwell, 2007) by Timothy Williamson develops my own view in greater detail concerning many of the topics covered in this book.

Philosophy: A Very Short Introduction (Oxford: Oxford University Press, 2002) by Edward Craig introduces various philosophers and philosophical topics rather than philosophical methods.

Articles in the online *Stanford Encyclopedia of Philosophy* (https://plato.stanford.edu) often make informative and up-to-date starting points for finding out more about philosophers and philosophical topics.

Chapter 1: Introduction

Descartes's writings on method can be found in *Descartes: Selected Philosophical Writings* (Cambridge: Cambridge University Press, 1988), translated by John Cottingham, Robert Stoothoff, and Dugald Murdoch.

Chapter 2 of *Knowledge: A Very Short Introduction* (Oxford: Oxford University Press, 2014) by Jennifer Nagel discusses scepticism.

Chapter 2: Starting from common sense

G.E. Moore, 'A defence of common sense', is in his *Philosophical Papers* (London: Routledge, reprinted 2010): 32–59.

Two attacks on common sense are J.M.E. McTaggart, 'The unreality of time', reprinted in *The Philosophy of Time* (Oxford: Oxford University Press, 1993): 23–34, edited by Robin Le Poidevin and Murray MacBeath; and Peter Unger, 'There are no ordinary things', *Synthese*, 41 (1979): 117–54.

Knowledge and Its Place in Nature (Oxford: Oxford University Press, 2nd edition, 2005) by Hilary Kornblith discusses knowledge as a common feature of animals.

Chapter 7 of my *Philosophy of Philosophy* (Oxford: Wiley-Blackwell, 2007) discusses evidence in philosophy.

Chapter 3: Disputing

For medieval oral disputations, see 'Obligationes' by Catarina Dutilh Novaes and Sara Uckelman in *The Cambridge Companion to Medieval Logic* (Cambridge: Cambridge University Press, 2016): 370–95, edited by Catarina Dutilh Novaes and Stephen Read.

Logic, Language-Games and Information (Oxford: Clarendon Press, 1973) by Jaakko Hintikka presents one approach to dialogue games in modern logic.

The dialogues by Plato, Galileo, and Hume are available in many editions.

The others referred to are *New Essays on Human Understanding* (Cambridge: Cambridge University Press, 2nd edition, 2008) by Gottfried Wilhelm Leibniz, translated and edited by Peter Remnant and Jonathan Bennett, in effect a long dialogue between Locke and Leibniz (guess who wins), and *Three Dialogues between Hylas and Philonous* (Indianapolis, IN: Hackett, 1979) by George Berkeley, edited by Robert Adams.

For discussion of the form, see *Philosophical Dialogues: Plato, Hume, Wittgenstein* (Oxford: Oxford University Press, 1995), edited by Timothy Smiley.

For an evolutionary theory of reason as a means of persuading others without being too easily persuaded oneself, see Hugo Mercier and Dan Sperber, *The Enigma of Reason* (Cambridge, MA: Harvard University Press, 2017).

I discuss the very technical dispute between generality absolutism and generality relativism in 'Everything', *Philosophical Perspectives*, 17 (2003): 415–65.

For dialogue and argument versions of the sorites paradox, see my *Vagueness* (London: Routledge, 1994), chapter 1.

My own venture into dialogue form is *Tetralogue: I'm Right, You're Wrong* (Oxford: Oxford University Press, 2015).

The zebra example is inspired by one in Fred Dretske's 'Epistemic operators', *Journal of Philosophy*, 67 (1970): 1007–23, discussed in chapter 7 of Nagel's *Knowledge: A Very Short Introduction* (Oxford: Oxford University Press, 2014).

Chapter 4: Clarifying terms

For Carnap's view, see 'Empiricism, semantics, and ontology' in his *Meaning and Necessity: A Study in Semantics and Modal Logic* (Chicago, IL: University of Chicago Press, 2nd edition, 1956): 205–21.

For Wittgenstein's view of philosophy, it is best to start with his philosophical practice, as in his *Philosophical Investigations* (Oxford: Wiley-Blackwell, 4th edition, 2009), edited by Peter Hacker and Joachim Schulte.

For a modern version of philosophy as conceptual analysis, see Frank Jackson, *From Metaphysics to Ethics: A Defence of Conceptual Analysis* (Oxford: Clarendon Press, 1998).

For philosophical issues around 'woman', see Sally Haslanger, 'The sex/gender distinction and the social construction of reality' in the *Routledge Companion to Feminist Philosophy* (New York: Routledge, 2017): 157–67, edited by Ann Garry, Serene Khader, and Alison Stone.

Gödel articulates his platonism in 'What is Cantor's continuum problem?' in his *Collected Works, Volume II: Publications 1938–1974* (Oxford: Oxford University Press, 2001): 254–70, edited by Solomon Feferman and others.

My objections to conceptual truth are explained at length in chapters 3 and 4 of my *Philosophy of Philosophy* (Oxford: Wiley-Blackwell, 2007).

Chapter 5: Doing thought experiments

For Dharmottara's case, see Jonathan Stoltz, 'Gettier and factivity in Indo-Tibetan epistemology', *Philosophical Quarterly*, 57 (2007): 394–415, and Jonardon Ganeri, *The Concealed Art of the Soul: Theories of the Self and Practices of Truth in Indian Ethics and Epistemology* (Oxford: Oxford University Press, 2007): 132–3; versions of the example go back several centuries before Dharmottara in Indian philosophy. Jennifer Nagel uses it and another ancient example in her discussion of the Gettier problem in chapter 4 of her *Knowledge: A Very Short Introduction* (Oxford: Oxford University Press, 2014). The paper that caused all the modern fuss is Edmund Gettier, 'Is justified true belief knowledge?', *Analysis*, 23 (1963): 121–3. For excruciating detail on the first wave of responses to Gettier, see Robert Shope, *The Analysis of Knowing: A Decade of Research* (Princeton, NJ: Princeton University Press, 1983). I defend the idea that knowledge is basic in *Knowledge and Its Limits* (Oxford: Oxford University Press, 2000).

The violinist case is in Judith Jarvis Thomson, 'A defense of abortion', *Philosophy and Public Affairs*, 1 (1971): 47–66.

For many more thought experiments, see Roy Sorensen, *Thought Experiments* (Oxford: Oxford University Press, 1998).

I analyse the structure of thought experiments in more detail in chapter 6 of my *Philosophy of Philosophy* (Oxford: Wiley-Blackwell, 2007).

Gyges' ring appears in book 2 of Plato's dialogue the *Republic*.

Zombies are discussed in David Chalmers, *The Conscious Mind: In Search of a Fundamental Theory* (Oxford: Oxford University Press, 1996).

The use of imagination to gain knowledge is explored in my 'Knowing and imagining' in *Knowledge Through Imagination* (Oxford: Oxford University Press, 2016): 113–23, edited by Amy Kind and Peter Kung.

For a positive take on the role of intuitions in thought experiments, see Jennifer Nagel, 'Intuitions and experiments: a defense of the case method in epistemology', *Philosophy and Phenomenological Research*, 85 (2012): 495–527. For a negative take, see Herman Cappelen, *Philosophy Without Intuitions* (Oxford: Oxford University Press, 2012).

The seminal article for the idea that verdicts on philosophical thought experiments may vary with ethnicity or gender was 'Normativity and epistemic intuitions' by Jonathan Weinberg, Shaun Nichols, and Stephen Stich, *Philosophical Topics*, 29 (2001): 429–60.

Experimental Philosophy: An Introduction (Cambridge: Polity, 2012) by Joshua Alexander is what it says. For the current state of play in that tradition, see *A Companion to Experimental Philosophy* (Oxford: Wiley-Blackwell, 2016), edited by Justin Sytsma and Wesley Buckwalter.

Chapter 6: Comparing theories

For a more extensive introductory discussion of physicalism, dualism, and related theories, see Jaegwon Kim, *Philosophy of Mind* (Boulder, CO: Westview, 3rd edition, 2010).

For relevant background in philosophy of science, see Samir Okasha, *Philosophy of Science: A Very Short Introduction* (Oxford: Oxford University Press, 2002).

Gilbert Harman, 'The inference to the best explanation', *Philosophical Review*, 74 (1965): 88–95, and Peter Lipton, *Inference to the Best Explanation* (London: Routledge, 2nd edition, 2004) are classic treatments of the subject.

On overfitting, see Malcolm Forster and Elliott Sober, 'How to tell when simpler, more unified, or less *ad hoc* theories will provide more accurate predictions', *British Journal for the Philosophy of Science*, 45 (1994): 1–34.

I discuss the theme of this chapter in more detail in 'Abductive philosophy', *Philosophical Forum*, 47 (2016): 263–80.

Chapter 7: Deducing

Logic: A Very Short Introduction (Oxford: Oxford University Press, 2000) by Graham Priest—a leading proponent of dialetheism—is accessible.

For an introduction to paradoxes that have motivated proposals to revise logic, see Mark Sainsbury, *Paradoxes* (Cambridge: Cambridge University Press, 3rd edition, 2009).

The quotation on induction comes from a 1907 essay, 'The regressive method of discovering the premises of mathematics', reprinted in Bertrand Russell, *Essays in Analysis* (London: George Allen & Unwin, 1973): 272–83, edited by Douglas Lackey. The quotation on logic and zoology comes from Russell's *Introduction to Mathematical Philosophy* (London: George Allen & Unwin, 1919): 169.

For the issues in modal logic raised at the end of the chapter, see chapter 1 of my *Modal Logic as Metaphysics* (Oxford: Oxford University Press, 2013).

Chapter 8: Using the history of philosophy

For an insightful but inconclusively argued diagnosis of the problem underlying the verification principle, see Willard Quine, 'Two dogmas of empiricism', *Philosophical Review*, 60 (1951): 20–43.

Thomas Kuhn, *The Structure of Scientific Revolutions* (Chicago, IL: University of Chicago Press, 2nd edition, 1970) is a good read.

For the work of Imre Lakatos, see his *Philosophical Papers, Volume 1: The Methodology of Scientific Research Programmes* (Cambridge: Cambridge University Press, 1978), edited by John Worrall and Gregory Currie.

Chapter 9: Using other fields

The ideal/non-ideal theory distinction is drawn in John Rawls, *A Theory of Justice* (Cambridge, MA: Harvard University Press, revised edition, 1999).

The relevant book by Evans-Pritchard is *Witchcraft, Oracles and Magic among the Azande* (Oxford: Clarendon Press, 1937).

On relativism, see Maria Baghramian, *Relativism* (London: Routledge, 2004); Paul Boghossian, *Fear of Knowledge: Against Relativism and Constructivism* (Oxford: Clarendon Press, 2006); and my *Tetralogue: I'm Right, You're Wrong* (Oxford: Oxford University Press, 2015).

The interaction of linguistics and philosophy of language can be observed in almost every chapter of *The Routledge Companion to Philosophy of Language* (London: Routledge, 2012), edited by Gillian Russell and Delia Graff Fara.

For the interaction of psychology and philosophy of perception, see *The Oxford Handbook of Philosophy of Perception* (Oxford: Oxford University Press, 2015), edited by Mohan Matthen.

For psychologically based objections to traditional philosophical conceptions of self-knowledge, see Peter Carruthers, *Opacity of Mind: An Integrative Theory of Self-Knowledge* (Oxford: Oxford University Press, 2011).

For decision theory, an area of extensive overlap between philosophy and theoretical economics and computer science, see Martin Peterson, *An Introduction to Decision Theory* (Cambridge: Cambridge University Press, 2nd edition, 2017).

For seminal work on epistemic logic, see Jaakko Hintikka, *Knowledge and Belief* (Ithaca, NY: Cornell University Press, 1962). For applications of epistemic logic to computer science and economics, see Ronald Fagin, Joseph Halpern, Yoram Moses, and Moshe Vardi, *Reasoning About Knowledge* (Cambridge, MA: MIT Press, 1995).

Several of the essays in Hilary Putnam, *Philosophical Papers, Volume 2: Mind, Language and Reality* (Cambridge: Cambridge University Press, 1979) discuss the relation between computers and minds. The 'computational theory of mind' is discussed in most works on philosophy of mind.

For an influential biological approach to some central questions of philosophy, see Ruth Garrett Millikan, *Language, Thought and Other Biological Categories: New Foundations for Realism* (Cambridge, MA: MIT Press, 1984).

For the problem posed by Einstein's theory of special relativity for a common view of time, see Hilary Putnam, 'Time and physical geometry', *Journal of Philosophy*, 64 (1967): 240–7).

Most contemporary work in philosophy of biology and philosophy of physics shows philosophy learning from the science, not just reflecting philosophically on it.

Chapter 10: Model-building

Michael Weisberg, *Simulation and Similarity: Using Models to Understand the World* (Oxford: Oxford University Press, 2013) is a good introduction to the philosophy of model-building.

Carnap developed his intensional semantics in his *Meaning and Necessity: A Study in Semantics and Modal Logic* (Chicago, IL: University of Chicago Press, 2nd edition, 1956).

My view of the topic is further explained in my 'Model-building in philosophy' in *Philosophy's Future: The Problem of Philosophical Progress* (Oxford: Wiley-Blackwell, 2017): 159–73, edited by Russell Blackford and Damien Broderick.

Index

Index

M

N

O

P